Dedicated to
The World's Greatest Strategist
Lord Krishna.

Contents

Case 1: Amazon -The E-Commerce Revolution 3
Case 2: Starbucks - Brewing Resilience 8
Case 3: Nike - Global Domination 13
Case 4: Tesla - Winning in Electric Market 20
Case 5: Netflix - Redefining Entertainment 26
Case 6: Microsoft - Adversity to Tech Giant 32
Case 7: Patagonia - Sustainability Pays Off 38
Case 8: Facebook - Privacy to Prosperity 43
Case 9: Apple - Setback to Comeback 48
Case 10: Louis Vuitton - Iconic Luxury Rise 53
Case 11: McDonald's - Reinventing Fast Food 58
Case 12: Ford - Struggles to Success 63
Case 13: Pfizer - Setbacks to Global Impact 67
Case 14: Google - Search Engine Supremacy 72
Case 15: Patagonia - Conscious Business Icon 76
Case 16: Airbnb - Hospitality Disruption 80
Case 17: Goldman Sachs - Scandal to Resilience 84
Case 18: Gucci - Global Luxury Icon 89
Case 19: Spotify - Music Streaming Empire 92
Case 20: Coca-Cola - Reigniting Growth 97
Case 21: Costco - Thriving with Uniqueness 102
Case 22: JPMorgan - Financial Crisis to Strength 107
Case 23: Samsung - Hardship to Leadership 113
Case 24: Intel - Disruption to Dominance 118
Case 25: LEGO - Building Blocks of Success 123
Case 26: eBay - Obsolescence to Leader 129
Case 27: Delta - Leading the Skies 135
Case 28: IBM - Adversity to Tech Powerhouse 141
Case 29: Alibaba - Global E-Commerce Empire 147

Case 1:
Amazon
The E-Commerce Revolution

Introduction: Amazon was founded in 1994 by Jeff Bezos, and initially, it was a modest online bookstore. The company grew rapidly, establishing itself as a pioneer in e-commerce. However, by the early 2000s, Amazon was not the thriving giant we know today. Despite its early success, it was still not profitable. Investors and skeptics began to question if the model would ever work, especially with so much competition on the horizon.

The Problem: By 2001, Amazon was in deep trouble. The dot-com bubble burst, and the financial climate shifted drastically. Amazon was burning through cash at an alarming rate and could not show profits despite high sales. The company faced an existential crisis – it was in debt, its stock price plummeting, and people were skeptical about online retail. Analysts predicted Amazon would not survive. Bezos's vision was challenged like never before.

The Situation Becomes Worse: As the crisis deepened, the situation grew even more critical. In an attempt to make up for the lack of profitability, Amazon tried expanding into other product categories. However, this led to overextension and logistical nightmares. Expanding too quickly stretched the company thin, making operations messy and customer experience inconsistent. As more players entered the market, Amazon's differentiation began to blur. The company wasn't just losing money; it was also losing the trust of its customers.

The Turning Point – Bold Moves: Realizing the situation was critical, Bezos made the decision to stick to his long-term vision, even at the cost of short-term losses. Amazon decided to focus on customer-centricity as the core of its business strategy. Investing heavily in infrastructure and technology, Amazon restructured its business to prioritize faster deliveries and better customer service, even if it meant more initial losses. Bezos doubled down on innovation, committing to reinvesting every dollar back into Amazon's growth, even as others were cutting back.

The Crisis Reaches Its Worst Point: Despite these changes, the situation continued to worsen. Competitors like Walmart and eBay were dominating in areas Amazon had not fully mastered. Amazon's stock kept falling, and some even speculated that the company would shut down. Yet, Bezos stayed focused on the long-term benefits of Prime, Amazon's subscription model, which promised to offer exclusive deals and fast delivery.

The Breakthrough: Then came The Breakthrough. In 2005, Amazon launched Amazon Prime, a service offering free two-day shipping for a fixed annual fee. This would transform the e-commerce space. Slowly but surely, customers began to flock to Amazon for the convenience and speed it provided. Additionally, the company diversified into other high-margin services like Amazon Web Services (AWS), further cementing its position as a leader in both retail and cloud computing.

The Ultimate Success: By 2010, Amazon was on a trajectory to become a global leader in e-commerce. Its Prime membership continued to skyrocket, AWS became a major revenue stream, and Amazon's shift toward being a technology-first company set it apart from other retailers. It went from being nearly bankrupt to becoming one of the most valuable companies in the world, reshaping the retail industry.

The Strategy:

1. Customer-Centric Focus: Amazon's primary focus became its customers, revolutionizing the online shopping experience with fast shipping, easy returns, and personalized recommendations.
2. Technology and Logistics Investments: Bezos invested in building cutting-edge infrastructure, from warehouses to AI-powered algorithms for better inventory management and quicker delivery.
3. Expansion and Diversification: Amazon expanded beyond books to almost every product category imaginable, with an emphasis on creating new services like Amazon Web Services (AWS), which turned into a major business unit.
4. Prime Subscription Model: The introduction of Amazon Prime helped

build customer loyalty and a steady revenue stream. The model of offering convenience, speed, and exclusive content led to an exponential rise in membership.

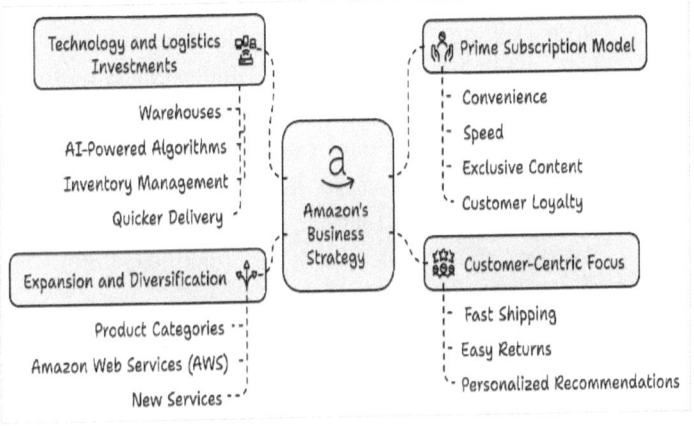

Key Takeaway:

"When faced with adversity, Amazon's resilience, focus on long-term goals, and willingness to make bold decisions created not only a path to survival but also one of the most powerful business transformations in history. The lesson: turn adversity into opportunity by staying customer-focused, investing in technology, and being ready to pivot when needed."

Case 2:
Starbucks
Brewing Resilience

Introduction: Starbucks, founded in 1971 in Seattle by three partners, was originally a small store selling high-quality coffee beans and equipment. In 1982, Howard Schultz joined and envisioned creating a "third place" between work and home. Schultz transformed Starbucks into a global coffeehouse chain, building an empire on premium coffee and unique customer experience. By the mid-2000s, Starbucks dominated the coffee industry worldwide.

The Problem: By 2007, Starbucks hit a major roadblock. The company, once known for innovation and a strong brand, began to lose its charm. The market became saturated with Starbucks locations, and the unique experience felt predictable. Competitors like Dunkin' Donuts and the rise of specialty coffee hurt Starbucks' market share. Loyal customers began seeking more authentic and affordable alternatives.

The Situation Becomes Worse: By 2008, Starbucks was facing its greatest crisis. The U.S. economy was in a recession, and people were cutting back on non-essential spending. Starbucks had overexpanded, opening too many stores in the same locations, undermining their own sales. The company's stock price plummeted, and many analysts believed the brand had lost its way. Schultz, who had stepped down as CEO in 2000, was brought back to reverse the declining fortunes of the company.

The Turning Point – Schultz's Bold Move: Upon returning as CEO, Schultz boldly closed 900 underperforming U.S. stores and focused on reinventing Starbucks' core—its coffee quality and customer experience. Schultz streamlined operations, emphasizing premium coffee and cutting back on non-core products like music and movies, which diluted the Starbucks experience.

He also revitalized the company's culture by introducing sustainability programs, focusing on ethically sourced coffee, better working conditions for employees (called "partners"), and greener stores.

The Crisis Reaches Its Worst Point: Despite these efforts, the company's turnaround was not immediate. As Starbucks closed stores, critics said it was a sign of decline rather than recovery. During the global financial crisis, consumers were still hesitant to spend money on premium-priced coffee. Starbucks was still facing high debt, and competitors were rapidly eating into its market share. Schultz's return did not immediately reverse the downward spiral, and the company's reputation as the "premium coffee chain" began to erode further.

The Breakthrough: In 2009, Schultz refocused Starbucks on customer loyalty and experience, transforming its stores into community hubs with free Wi-Fi, where people could relax, work, and connect. Emphasizing the experience over the product, Starbucks introduced a diverse range of offerings, including healthier options and seasonal drinks, to cater to varying consumer preferences. The brand also embraced digital innovation by launching a mobile app for seamless ordering and payments. By 2010, these strategic changes led to Starbucks' recovery and renewed growth.

The Ultimate Success: Starbucks not only survived the economic crisis but emerged as a stronger, more relevant brand. The company now had over 30,000 stores worldwide, a loyalty program with millions of members, and a thriving digital ecosystem. Starbucks' focus on sustainability, innovation, and customer experience has allowed it to maintain a dominant position in the coffee industry, even in the face of increasing competition.

The Strategy:

1. Back to Basics – Simplifying Focus: Schultz simplified the product line, emphasizing coffee quality and exceptional customer service.
2. Cultural and Operational Overhaul: Starbucks reinvested in employee welfare, fostering a culture aligned with its mission and values.
3. Digital Innovation and Loyalty: The Starbucks mobile app enhanced convenience, loyalty, and rewarded regular customers.
4. Sustainability and Ethical Sourcing: Ethically sourced coffee and environmental sustainability attracted conscientious consumers.

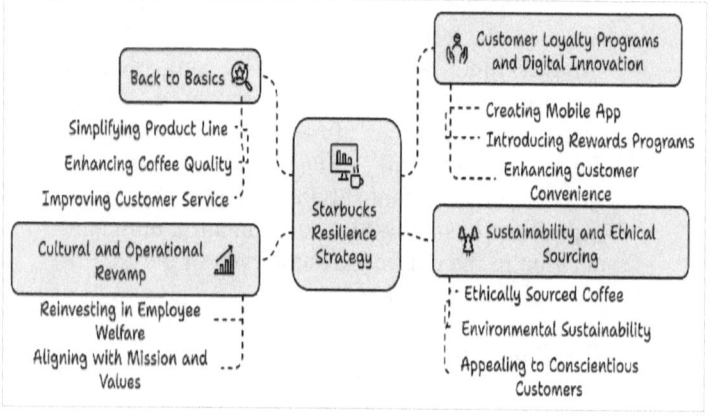

Key Takeaway:

"Starbucks' story teaches us that even when facing immense challenges—whether economic downturns, overexpansion, or competition—returning to the core values of quality, customer experience, and innovation is the key to long-term success. The lesson is clear: when adversity strikes, reassess and reinvest in your foundation, evolve with the times, and continue to innovate."

Case 3:
Nike
Global Domination

Introduction: Nike, originally founded in 1964 as Blue Ribbon Sports by Bill Bowerman and Phil Knight, began its journey as a small distributor of Japanese running shoes. In its humble beginnings, Knight famously sold shoes from the trunk of his car at athletic events. However, the company transformed dramatically with the introduction of the iconic swoosh logo (a simple, curved checkmark) and its emphasis on performance-oriented athletic footwear. This vision propelled Nike into the spotlight, eventually becoming a global leader in the sports apparel industry.

By the 1980s, Nike had become an industry giant, revolutionizing performance gear for athletes. Its success was amplified through strategic endorsements, most notably with basketball legend Michael Jordan. The 1985 launch of the Air Jordan line elevated Nike, cementing its place as a symbol of athletic excellence and innovation. The brand redefined how people approached sports and fitness as a lifestyle.

The Problem: By the late 1990s and early 2000s, Nike faced significant challenges. Despite its earlier triumphs, the company began losing ground to competitors like Adidas and Reebok. These rivals gained traction in the market, offering innovative products and carving out niches that Nike initially overlooked. Simultaneously, Nike's reputation suffered as allegations of unethical labor practices in its overseas factories surfaced. These accusations, particularly concerning factories in Asia, drew widespread criticism and tainted Nike's image in Western markets, where social responsibility had become increasingly important.

Adding to its struggles, the athleisure trend was rapidly growing, with consumers seeking versatile, stylish athletic wear that could transition from workouts to everyday life. Nike's initial failure to capitalize on this shift allowed competitors to seize the opportunity, further eroding its market dominance. The brand began to seem disconnected from changing consumer expectations, and its once-loyal customer base started exploring alternatives. Sales dropped, and analysts questioned whether Nike could reclaim its former glory.

The Situation Worsens: Nike's struggles deepened as critics pointed out outdated designs and limited innovation. Competitors like Adidas thrived with products such as Boost technology, while Reebok targeted niches like CrossFit. This external competition, combined with internal challenges and negative public perception, caused Nike's stock price to drop. Once an aspirational brand, Nike now seemed stagnant, forcing the company to confront its shortcomings and adapt to a rapidly changing market.

The Turning Point – Rebranding and Cultural Shift: In 2008, Nike made a bold decision to reinvent itself under the leadership of CEO Mark Parker. The company undertook a comprehensive rebranding effort that focused on three key areas: sustainability, innovation, and digital transformation. Through initiatives like Nike Better World, the brand committed to using eco-friendly materials and ethical labor practices, addressing the criticism it faced over its previous operations.

At the same time, Nike revitalized its product line, launching cutting-edge innovations like Nike Flyknit shoes. These lightweight, comfortable shoes were created using sustainable production methods, showcasing Nike's dedication to blending performance with environmental responsibility. By doubling down on product development, Nike demonstrated that it could still lead the industry in innovation.

Additionally, Nike embraced the athleisure trend, creating stylish, functional apparel that catered to a broader audience. By integrating fashion with athletic performance, Nike appealed to consumers seeking versatility in their wardrobes. This shift allowed the brand to recapture a share of the growing market.

The Digital Revolution: Nike also became a pioneer in digital fitness. The launch of platforms like Nike Training Club and Nike Run Club connected the brand to consumers on a personal level, fostering loyalty and engagement. These apps not only offered workout guidance but also built a sense of community among users, enabling Nike to tap into the global fitness culture.

Through targeted digital marketing campaigns, Nike reached a new generation of customers. Social media and influencer collaborations became integral to its strategy, allowing Nike to remain relevant in an increasingly digital world. Campaigns like "Just Do It" were reimagined to emphasize individual empowerment, resonating deeply with audiences.

The Crisis Reaches Its Worst Point: Despite these strategic moves, Nike's path to recovery was not easy. The 2008 financial crisis posed significant challenges, as consumers tightened their spending on non-essential goods. Nike's premium products were often seen as a luxury, making it difficult for the company to maintain sales momentum.

Public skepticism over Nike's labor practices and environmental impact persisted. The brand faced scrutiny at every turn, forcing it to be more transparent and accountable in its operations. These struggles underscored the magnitude of the transformation Nike needed to undergo.

The Breakthrough: By 2010, Nike's commitment to sustainability and innovation began yielding results. Eco-friendly products like the Nike Flyknit proved that sustainability could align with exceptional performance, helping Nike regain its market leadership. These efforts won over both critics and customers, reaffirming Nike's position as an industry innovator.

The reinvigorated "Just Do It" campaign resonated deeply, inspiring consumers to push boundaries while leveraging digital platforms and influencers to create authentic, empowering narratives. With diversification into athleisure and a focus on digital fitness, Nike's resurgence was solidified, transforming it into a cultural force beyond sportswear by 2015.

The Strategy:

1. Rebranding for Sustainability and Ethical Responsibility: Nike addressed criticism by adopting eco-friendly materials and improving labor practices.
2. Digital Transformation: The brand connected with consumers through fitness apps and digital marketing, fostering deeper engagement.
3. Innovation and Product Development: Cutting-edge designs like Flyknit balanced performance with sustainability.
4. Adapting to the Athleisure Trend: Nike diversified its offerings to meet consumer demand for versatile, fashionable athletic wear.
5. Reinvigorating the "Just Do It" Campaign: A renewed focus on empowerment resonated with a new generation of customers.

Business Case Studies: The Journey from Adversity to Opportunity

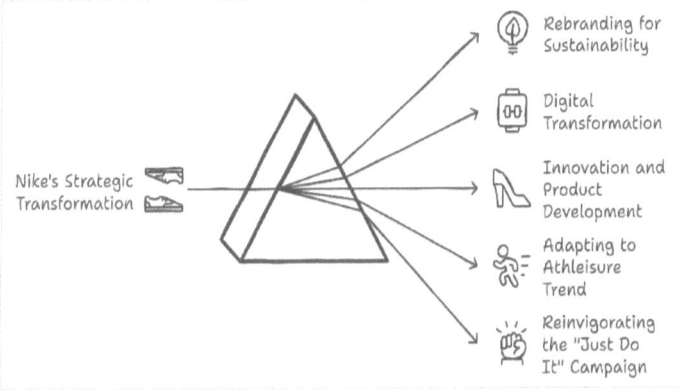

Key Takeaway:

Nike's journey underscores the importance of embracing change and staying true to core values. Even in the face of adversity, companies can thrive by innovating, adapting to market shifts, and connecting with their audience. Nike's transformation is a testament to the power of reinvention and resilience.

Case 4:
Tesla
Winning in Electric Market

Introduction: In 2003, Tesla Motors was founded by a group of engineers, including Elon Musk, with the bold vision to revolutionize the automobile industry by creating electric vehicles (EVs) that were not only environmentally friendly but also high-performance and desirable. The company's mission was clear: to accelerate the world's transition to sustainable energy.

Despite the early promise of EVs, the auto industry was dominated by gasoline-powered vehicles, and the electric car market was largely seen as niche and impractical. In 2008, Tesla introduced its first production car, the Roadster, a high-end sports car. However, its steep price tag made it out of reach for most consumers, and the company faced mounting challenges to remain afloat. Tesla was still an unknown name in the crowded automotive market, and doubts about its sustainability began to grow.

The Problem: As Tesla prepared to launch its Model S in 2012, it faced severe financial troubles amidst global economic uncertainty. Rapidly burning cash, Tesla struggled with a funding crisis and skepticism over its ability to scale electric vehicle production for the mass market.

Technical hurdles added to the strain, with battery issues and manufacturing delays causing negative press and frustrating early adopters. The company's stock price plummeted, casting doubt on Tesla's ability to secure its future in a volatile automotive industry.

The Situation Becomes Worse: As the financial crisis deepened, Tesla was on the verge of collapse. By 2013, it struggled to meet production targets, and the Model X SUV faced delays. Investors wondered if Tesla had taken on too much, given its production issues and cash burn.

The electric car industry was in its infancy, and automakers were skeptical about EVs' long-term potential. Meanwhile, gasoline-powered vehicles dominated, and consumers were hesitant about electric cars due to range anxiety and high costs.

The Crisis Reaches Its Worst Point: By 2014, Tesla held less than 1% of the global car market, with many speculating it would soon run out of money. Production remained limited, critics dismissed its scaling plans as "ambitious dreams," and competitors entering the electric vehicle market threatened Tesla's pioneering position. As financial reserves diminished, Elon Musk admitted he came so close to bankruptcy that he had to secure investor support to keep Tesla afloat, casting doubt on the company's bold mission for sustainable automobiles.

The Breakthrough – Turning the Impossible into Possible: In 2015, Tesla launched the Model 3, an affordable electric car aimed at bringing electric vehicles to the masses. Its success was critical for Tesla's survival. The company redefined its manufacturing process, focusing on mass production by expanding capacity and fine-tuning gigafactories, moving beyond luxury cars. Tesla also innovated in battery technology and energy storage, with products like the Powerwall strengthening its position as a clean energy leader. Musk's introduction of Autopilot advanced autonomous driving, giving Tesla a significant technological edge.

By 2017, Tesla made significant progress in its mission to create affordable electric cars for all. The Model 3 entered full-scale production, with Tesla meeting its targets. The company built the world's largest battery gigafactory in Nevada, which boosted investor confidence and showcased Tesla's ability to scale for mass-market electric vehicles.

The Company Rises Again: By 2020, Tesla had become the world's most valuable automaker in terms of market capitalization, surpassing General Motors and Ford. The company had not only survived its near-collapse but had transformed the automotive industry with its electric vehicle technology. Tesla's cars were no longer considered niche products, but a mainstream alternative to gas-powered vehicles. The company's stock price soared, and Tesla became a symbol of innovation and resilience in the tech and automotive sectors.

Tesla's story showed that adversity can lead to breakthrough innovation when a company stays focused on its long-term vision. By embracing failure as part of the process and relentlessly pursuing technological innovation, Tesla emerged as an industry leader.

The Strategy:

1. Innovation Overcoming Adversity: Tesla's focus on cutting-edge technology, especially battery innovation and autonomous driving, helped it build a competitive advantage in the electric vehicle market.
2. Scalability of Production: Tesla invested in Gigafactories to scale production and reduce costs, making electric vehicles affordable for the mass market.
3. Focus on the Mission: Elon Musk's commitment to sustainability and clean energy guided Tesla through challenges, helping it persevere during financial hardship.
4. Disrupting Auto Manufacturing: Tesla revolutionized car design with a direct-to-consumer model and software-driven updates, positioning itself as an industry disruptor.
5. Customer Loyalty: Tesla built a loyal customer base by delivering premium experiences, leveraging word-of-mouth, and engaging customers uniquely.

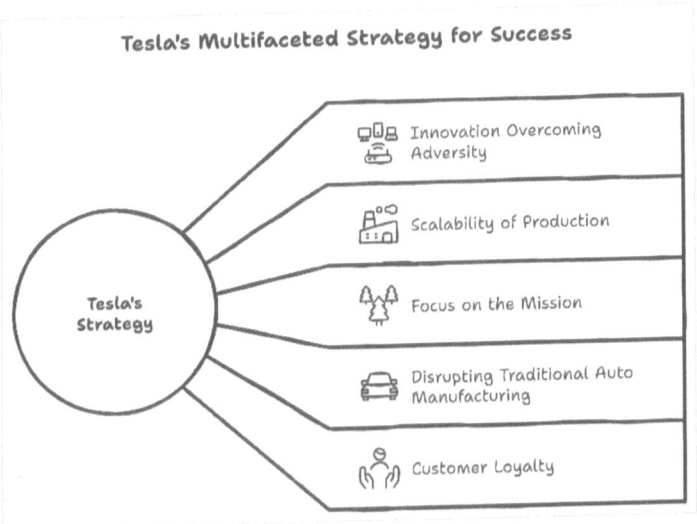

Key Takeaway:

"Tesla's rise from near collapse to global dominance teaches us that embracing adversity, staying true to a long-term vision, and continuously innovating can transform a company and even an industry. Tesla didn't just survive the storm; it turned the challenges it faced into opportunities to redefine the future of transportation."

Case 5:
Netflix
Rewriting the Rules of Entertainment

Introduction: In 1997, Reed Hastings and Marc Randolph founded Netflix as a DVD rental-by-mail service, a revolutionary idea at the time that sought to eliminate the inconvenience of visiting physical rental stores. For a monthly fee, customers could rent DVDs, which would be mailed to their doorsteps, changing the way people consumed movies and TV shows.

In the early 2000s, Netflix's subscription-based model became a game-changer in the entertainment industry, offering people convenience and a vast catalog of movies and TV shows. However, despite the initial success, the company faced fierce competition from industry giants like Blockbuster and Hollywood Video, who dominated the movie rental space. While Netflix's business model seemed to be gaining traction, Blockbuster was still the dominant player, and Netflix's future remained uncertain.

The Problem: In 2007, Netflix faced its first major crisis when it realized that the market for DVD rentals was shrinking. More and more customers were moving toward digital streaming, and the company was caught at a crossroads. With Netflix's core business tied to physical DVD rentals, the company had to make a bold decision. In an age of internet connectivity, the future seemed to belong to digital streaming. But Netflix wasn't equipped to make that transition yet. At this time, the company was struggling to adapt to this new trend and faced the risk of falling behind.

The Situation Becomes Worse: By 2011, Netflix made a controversial move by separating its DVD rental and streaming services into two brands: Netflix and Qwikster. This confused customers, damaged its brand, and caused significant subscriber losses. Simultaneously, Netflix faced growing competition from Hulu and Amazon Prime Video as the industry rapidly shifted to digital consumption. Its stock price plummeted, and analysts questioned its viability, viewing it as a niche service unlikely to compete against giants with greater financial resources. Meanwhile, major players like HBO and Amazon were heavily investing in content, further threatening Netflix's position.

The Crisis Reaches Its Worst Point: In 2012, Netflix was in deep trouble. The company was struggling with a massive customer backlash due to the Qwikster fiasco, and its stock price had dropped by over 80% from its peak in 2011. Despite attempts to improve, the company was unable to retain its existing subscriber base and had to rethink its strategy entirely. The shift to streaming wasn't happening fast enough, and Netflix was still deeply reliant on licensing movies and TV shows from third-party content providers. It seemed that Netflix's moment of success was coming to an end.

The Breakthrough – Turning the Impossible into Possible: In 2013, Netflix shifted from being just a streaming platform to a content creator, starting with its first original series, House of Cards, an instant hit. This strategy gave Netflix control over its content and attracted millions of new subscribers with exclusive, original shows.

By 2016, Netflix was fully committed to producing original movies, documentaries, and TV shows that gained global popularity. Its investment in high-quality content expanded its reach, transforming the company into a global entertainment powerhouse. By 2018, Netflix surpassed 100 million subscribers, doubling by 2020. Winning Emmy Awards solidified its status in the entertainment industry. This shift to original content helped Netflix stand out in a crowded market, ensuring its dominance with a growing catalog of award-winning content.

The Company Rises Again:

By 2020, Netflix had become the undisputed leader in the streaming industry, with over 200 million subscribers worldwide. It transformed from a struggling DVD rental business to the largest subscription-based streaming service, revolutionizing entertainment consumption. Netflix positioned itself as the go-to platform for exclusive, high-quality content, producing acclaimed originals like Stranger Things, The Crown, and Narcos. Its innovative content strategy, aggressive global expansion, and focus on exceptional user experience kept Netflix ahead of the curve, solidifying its role as the future of entertainment.

The Strategy:

1. Pivot to Streaming: Recognizing declining DVD demand, Netflix shifted focus to digital streaming, embracing the future of entertainment.
2. Content Ownership: By investing in original content, Netflix gained a competitive edge, reducing reliance on third-party providers.
3. Global Expansion: Netflix strategically expanded services globally, localizing content and catering to diverse audiences, building a massive global subscriber base.
4. Data-Driven Approach: Netflix used analytics to understand viewer preferences and tailor recommendations, enhancing user experience and retention.
5. Disruption through Innovation: Netflix disrupted the entertainment industry with a flexible, affordable subscription model, offering ad-free, on-demand viewing.
6. Focus on Quality Content: Netflix became a content powerhouse, creating award-winning original shows that captivated global audiences.

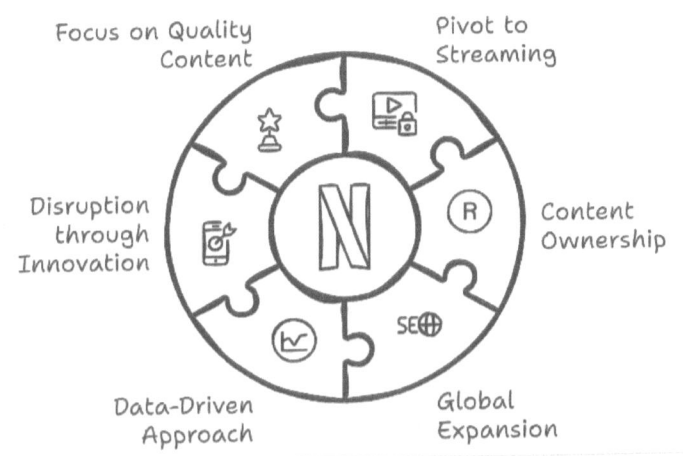

Key Takeaway:

"Netflix's journey from being a DVD rental service to a global streaming giant teaches us that embracing change, disrupting traditional models, and investing in innovation can help a company not only survive but thrive. By betting on original content and global expansion, Netflix turned adversity into its greatest opportunity, forever changing the entertainment landscape."

Case 6:
Microsoft
Adversity to Tech Giant

Introduction: Founded in 1975 by Bill Gates and Paul Allen, Microsoft revolutionized the personal computing industry with its Windows operating system and Office software suite. By the late 1990s, Microsoft had cemented its position as the dominant player in the tech industry. However, despite its immense success, the company faced significant challenges in the early 2000s that threatened its future.

At the peak of its dominance, Microsoft was still largely reliant on its Windows operating system and Office software, while other companies were starting to embrace the internet and the rise of mobile technology. The company faced growing pressure to evolve and innovate beyond its existing products, and failure to adapt could cost them everything.

The Problem: By 2000, Microsoft faced a turning point as the rise of the internet and companies like Google and Apple threatened its dominance in tech. New business models emerged with the internet boom, and companies embraced cloud computing—a shift Microsoft was slow to follow.

Apple's strides with the iPhone established a mobile ecosystem that dominated globally, while Microsoft struggled in the mobile space. Efforts like Windows Mobile failed to gain traction as the market moved toward smartphones. Meanwhile, Google's rise in search and advertising directly challenged Microsoft's core software business. By 2005, Microsoft's stock stagnated, and its growth rate slowed significantly.

The Situation Becomes Worse: Microsoft's inability to adapt to the mobile and cloud computing revolutions put it at a severe disadvantage. Its main competitor, Apple, had already launched the iPhone in 2007, and the world was rapidly shifting towards mobile computing. Microsoft's attempts to compete with Apple in the mobile market with products like Windows Phone proved unsuccessful, and the company continued to lose ground in the consumer tech space.

In the mid-2000s, Google's dominance in search, advertising, and cloud computing also posed a major threat. Microsoft's internet explorer was quickly losing market share to Google's Chrome browser, and its online services were struggling to keep up with Google's offerings like Gmail and Google Docs. Microsoft seemed to be losing relevance in the new digital age.

The Crisis Reaches Its Worst Point: By the early 2010s, Microsoft was in danger of becoming a legacy tech company. Its stock price had stagnated, and it was largely seen as a company of the past, lagging behind the innovators of Silicon Valley. Microsoft's failure to adapt to the mobile and cloud revolutions seemed to signal its eventual decline.

In 2012, Microsoft made a high-profile but costly mistake by launching Windows 8, an operating system that alienated users with its radical interface change. The product flopped, and Microsoft's position in the tech world seemed increasingly fragile.

The Breakthrough – Rewriting the Playbook: In 2014, Microsoft appointed Satya Nadella as CEO, marking a transformative shift. Nadella envisioned Microsoft as a cloud-first, mobile-first company, emphasizing cloud computing and open-source technologies.

He revitalized Azure, positioning it as a strong competitor to Amazon's AWS, and focused on mobile applications, acquiring Nokia's mobile business in 2014. The $26 billion LinkedIn acquisition in 2016 expanded Microsoft's reach into professional markets, aligning with its cloud-first strategy.

Nadella's leadership reshaped Microsoft's culture, fostering innovation and collaboration. By 2017, the company regained momentum, achieving record profits in cloud and enterprise divisions.

The Company Rises Again: Today, Microsoft leads in cloud computing, with Azure competing closely with AWS. Revenue now comes from cloud computing, enterprise software, and LinkedIn. Its stock has soared, making Microsoft one of the world's most valuable companies.

Satya Nadella's leadership marks one of business history's greatest comebacks. By prioritizing cloud and mobile, Microsoft not only overcame its crisis but emerged stronger than ever.

The Strategy:

1. Embrace Change: Microsoft's ability to embrace cloud computing and mobile technologies allowed it to stay relevant in an era dominated by mobile-first businesses.
2. Leadership Change: The appointment of Satya Nadella brought fresh leadership and a new vision, focusing on a cloud-first approach and shifting away from legacy software.
3. Strategic Acquisitions: Microsoft made key acquisitions, such as LinkedIn and Nokia, to build its cloud and mobile capabilities and expand into new markets.
4. Focus on Enterprise Solutions: The company shifted its focus to providing enterprise solutions and cloud infrastructure services, making Azure a key part of its growth.
5. Cultural Shift: Under Nadella, Microsoft adopted a more collaborative and growth-oriented culture, encouraging innovation across departments.
6. Customer-Centric Approach: Microsoft began prioritizing customer needs and integrating open-source solutions, enabling the company to better serve its diverse customer base.

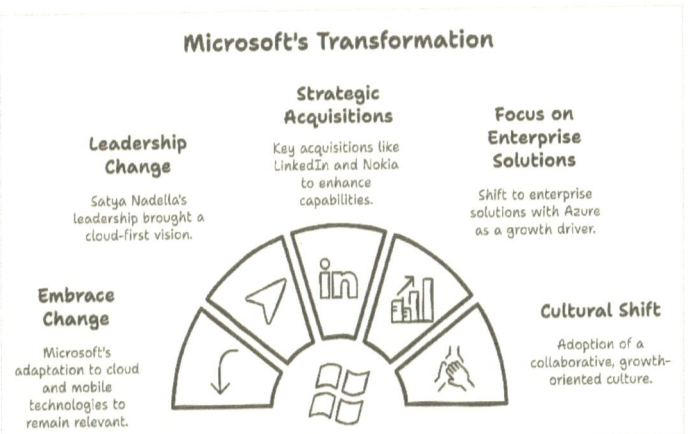

Key Takeaway:

"Microsoft's transformation from a stagnating tech giant to a cloud powerhouse highlights the importance of embracing change, adapting to market shifts, and investing in innovation. By making bold decisions and focusing on the future, Microsoft turned its adversity into opportunity and solidified its place as a leader in the tech industry."

Case 7:
Patagonia
Sustainability Pays Off

Introduction: Patagonia, a renowned outdoor apparel brand, has long been known for its commitment to sustainability and environmentalism. Founded in 1973 by Yvon Chouinard, the company was built on the values of outdoor adventure, conservation, and responsibility. However, by the early 2000s, the company found itself facing accusations of "greenwashing," or misleading consumers about the environmental impact of its products.

The Problem: Despite Patagonia's authentic efforts to protect the environment, the company was criticized for not doing enough. Competitors had jumped on the sustainability bandwagon, creating confusion in the marketplace. Patagonia's efforts seemed to be under threat as consumers began questioning the sincerity of corporate environmental claims. If Patagonia didn't address the mounting pressure from both its customers and critics, its reputation could be irreparably damaged.

The Situation Becomes Worse: As the demand for sustainable products soared, Patagonia's early efforts to champion environmental causes were getting lost in a sea of competing green claims. Other companies were marketing similar environmental products, but without the authentic backing that Patagonia had always stood for. The rise of digital marketing and social media also gave critics a louder voice, making it harder for Patagonia to defend its efforts in a transparent way.

The Crisis Reaches Its Worst Point: By the mid-2000s, Patagonia's brand was at risk. Environmental organizations and watchdog groups were publicly questioning the company's sincerity, while consumers were demanding stronger proof of real sustainability. The company's loyal following was beginning to falter as Patagonia faced the critical choice of either adapting or risking a long-term image crisis.

The Breakthrough - Rewriting the Playbook: Patagonia didn't shy away from the controversy. Instead, the company doubled down on its values. The first step was full transparency. Patagonia opened up its production process and supply chain to the public, disclosing both its successes and failures in creating sustainable products. This honesty helped Patagonia regain its trust with the public.

Patagonia also implemented ambitious initiatives, such as the Worn Wear program, which encouraged customers to buy second-hand items and trade in their old Patagonia gear for store credit. By reducing waste and promoting product longevity, Patagonia strengthened its position as a true environmental leader. The company also began donating 1% of its sales to environmental causes, an effort that resonated strongly with its eco-conscious audience.

The Company Rises Again: Patagonia's proactive approach to sustainability, including its transparent business practices and commitment to reducing environmental harm, helped it reclaim and even strengthen its reputation. The company's investments in sustainable materials and commitment to activism aligned with the growing demand for responsible business practices, and Patagonia became a model for businesses seeking to merge profitability with purpose.

The Strategy

1. Transparency and Accountability: Patagonia opened its supply chain and production process to the public, which established trust and credibility.
2. Innovative Programs: The company launched the Worn Wear initiative to encourage product reuse, repair, and reduce waste, addressing environmental concerns head-on.
3. Activism and Advocacy: Patagonia committed 1% of its sales to environmental causes, building stronger ties with the environmental community and proving its authenticity.
4. Focus on Sustainable Materials: The brand invested heavily in using organic cotton, recycled polyester, and other environmentally friendly materials in its products.
5. Customer Engagement: Patagonia built a strong relationship with its customers, not just through marketing, but by involving them in the sustainability journey.

Key Takeaway

"Patagonia's rise from the brink of a reputation crisis to becoming a leader in sustainable business practices illustrates the power of transparency, authenticity, and a steadfast commitment to values. By aligning profit-making with purpose and involving customers in its mission, Patagonia not only survived adversity but turned it into an opportunity for growth and impact."

Case 8:
Facebook
Privacy to Prosperity

Introduction: Facebook, founded in 2004 by Mark Zuckerberg and his college roommates, quickly grew into one of the most influential platforms in the world. By 2010, it had become the go-to social network, boasting over 1 billion users globally. However, behind its success, Facebook faced challenges surrounding user privacy, data protection, and its growing influence on politics and society.

The Problem: In 2018, Facebook was hit by one of its biggest scandals: the Cambridge Analytica data breach. It was revealed that personal data from millions of Facebook users had been harvested without consent by a third-party app and sold to political consulting firms. This created a massive privacy crisis, with users and governments worldwide questioning Facebook's ability to protect its users' data.

The company's stock plummeted, and its reputation took a serious hit. Legislators in the U.S. and Europe began investigating Facebook's data practices, and the company was slapped with multiple lawsuits. For a while, it seemed like Facebook's dominance might be challenged, and it was unclear how the company could recover.

The Situation Becomes Worse: Following the scandal, Facebook faced backlash from users, advertisers, and regulators. Beyond data protection issues, it was accused of spreading fake news, enabling political manipulation, and harming societal well-being.

Facebook's platform became associated with misinformation, hate speech, and divisive content, fueling public distrust. In 2019, advertiser protests and regulatory scrutiny escalated, with privacy violations threatening Facebook's user-data-driven business model.

The Crisis Reaches Its Worst Point: By 2019, Facebook had lost its trust among many of its users, and its ability to collect and monetize personal data came under increasing scrutiny. As global users demanded more privacy, competitors like Snapchat, TikTok, and others started gaining popularity. Facebook's growth began slowing down, and it seemed like a matter of time before new regulations or competitors could replace it as the dominant platform.

The Breakthrough - Turning Adversity into Opportunity: Instead of folding under pressure, Mark Zuckerberg took decisive action. He acknowledged Facebook's mistakes and vowed to prioritize privacy. Facebook overhauled its privacy policies, introduced better data protection tools, and invested in building a more transparent, user-centric platform.

To address trust issues, Facebook launched the "Privacy Checkup" tool for better user control. The company rebranded as more than a social network, introducing the slogan "More Together" to focus on meaningful connections.

Additionally, Facebook expanded by acquiring Instagram and WhatsApp, strengthening its ecosystem and diversifying its offerings in photo sharing, messaging, and e-commerce.

The Strategy

1. Refocusing on Privacy: Facebook acknowledged shortcomings and made privacy its top priority, rebuilding trust with users and regulators.
2. Investing in AI and Content Moderation: Facebook invested in AI to detect and remove harmful content, misinformation, and hate speech, improving user experience and platform safety.
3. Acquisitions and Diversification: Acquiring Instagram, WhatsApp, and Oculus diversified Facebook's business model, reducing reliance on a single platform.
4. Rebranding and Communication: Facebook repositioned itself as a platform for "connecting people" and shifted its narrative from a social network to a tech company committed to privacy and societal impact.
5. Enhanced Regulatory Compliance: Facebook strengthened compliance with global data protection laws, including GDPR, to avoid penalties and establish itself as a leader in digital privacy.

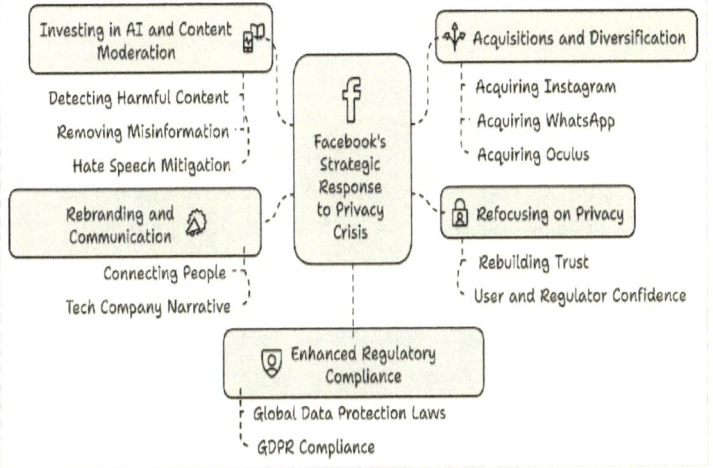

Key Takeaway

"Facebook's transformation from a privacy crisis to a global tech leader highlights the power of self-correction, innovation, and adaptability. By confronting its mistakes head-on, diversifying its services, and improving user privacy, Facebook not only survived the storm but turned adversity into the opportunity to expand its influence further."

Case 9:
Apple
Setback to Comeback

Introduction: Apple, founded in 1976 by Steve Jobs, Steve Wozniak, and Ronald Wayne, had been at the forefront of technological innovation for decades. By the early 2000s, Apple was known for revolutionizing consumer electronics with the iMac, iPod, iPhone, and iPad. However, despite its early success, Apple faced a near-collapse in the late 1990s, before being revived by Steve Jobs' return to the company in 1997.

The Problem: In the late 1990s, Apple faced near bankruptcy, losing its edge in the personal computer market. Its once-iconic products were obsolete, market share was shrinking, and profits were scarce. Unprofitable ventures like the Newton PDA and expensive hardware and software compared to affordable Windows PCs further worsened its position. Apple seemed destined to lose its standing as a major technology player.

The Situation Becomes Worse: As Apple continued to lose ground in the market, the company was forced to make significant cost-cutting measures. Jobs, upon his return to Apple, realized that the company had overextended itself and needed to refocus on its core strengths.

The company was not only dealing with its financial struggles but also with an identity crisis. Apple's once loyal customer base was dwindling, and competitors like Dell and Microsoft dominated the market with cheaper and more accessible products. Jobs knew that without drastic change, Apple would soon cease to exist.

The Breakthrough - Turning Adversity into Opportunity: In 1997, Steve Jobs made the bold decision to streamline Apple's product line, cutting down on unnecessary offerings and focusing on the core product strategy. He famously said, "We need to simplify. We need to make the products more beautiful, more useful, and more affordable."

In 1998, Apple introduced the iMac, a revolutionary product that combined cutting-edge design with ease of use. The iMac was an instant success, restoring Apple's image as an innovative company.

The real game-changer came in 2001 with the launch of the iPod, followed by the iPhone in 2007. Apple transformed itself into a company that didn't just make computers – it became a leader in mobile devices, digital music, and later, wearables. By focusing on design, user experience, and ecosystem integration, Apple revolutionized entire industries, moving from near bankruptcy to one of the most valuable companies in the world.

The Strategy

1. Refocusing on Core Competencies: Steve Jobs simplified Apple's product line and concentrated on quality, design, and user experience, eliminating unnecessary distractions.
2. Design and Innovation: Apple redefined the concept of product design, with an emphasis on aesthetics, functionality, and ease of use, which set Apple products apart from the competition.
3. Vertical Integration and Ecosystem Development: Apple created a closed

ecosystem of hardware, software, and services (like iTunes, App Store, and iCloud), providing seamless integration and fostering customer loyalty.

4. Brand and Marketing Excellence: Apple invested heavily in marketing, making its products synonymous with innovation, quality, and prestige. The brand became aspirational and influential.

5. Expansion into New Markets: Apple's foray into mobile phones (iPhone) and portable music players (iPod) allowed it to diversify its offerings and capitalize on emerging markets, strengthening its market position.

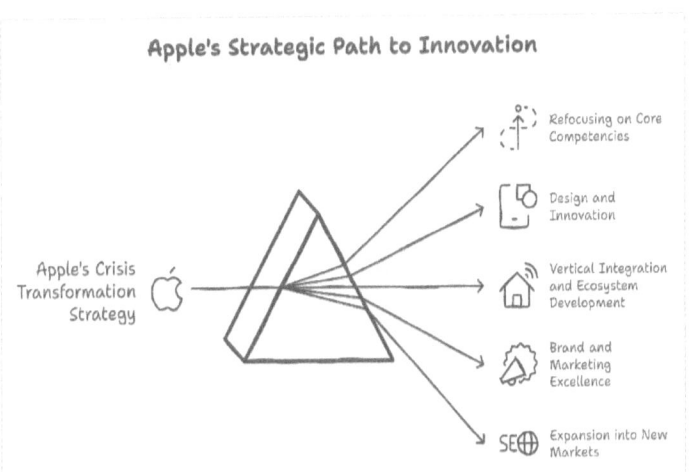

Key Takeaway

"Apple's remarkable recovery from the brink of bankruptcy to global dominance is a testament to the power of innovation, strategic focus, and brand loyalty. By simplifying its operations, prioritizing design, and creating a seamless ecosystem, Apple transformed adversity into opportunity and became an industry leader once again."

Case 10:
Louis Vuitton
Iconic Luxury Rise

Introduction: Louis Vuitton, founded in 1854 by the French designer Louis Vuitton, quickly became synonymous with luxury luggage and accessories. Over the decades, the brand expanded its offerings to include handbags, clothing, shoes, and fragrances, becoming a global symbol of high-end fashion. By the 20th century, Louis Vuitton had solidified itself as a status symbol, and its products were coveted by the world's elite.

The Problem: By the 1980s, Louis Vuitton faced a major problem. Its once-exclusive products suffered from widespread imitation, with counterfeit goods flooding the market and damaging its prestige. While the luxury goods industry thrived in the 1980s and 1990s, Louis Vuitton lagged behind competitors in innovation and diversification. Though its traditional monogrammed products remained popular, the company's failure to adapt to changing consumer preferences threatened its future.

The Situation Becomes Worse: The rise of counterfeit goods put Louis Vuitton's identity at risk. The brand became synonymous with cheap imitations, and despite efforts to combat counterfeiters, the damage to the luxury image was done. By the late 1990s, Louis Vuitton's market share was shrinking. Its core customer base was eroding, and competitors like Gucci and Prada were stealing the spotlight with more trendy and youthful designs.

Louis Vuitton's inability to reach younger, more diverse markets and its lack of innovation in product design further contributed to its downward spiral. It was clear that unless the brand reinvented itself, it would lose its position as a leading luxury brand.

The Breakthrough - Turning Adversity into Opportunity: Louis Vuitton turned its crisis into opportunity by embracing innovation, exclusivity, and collaboration with contemporary artists. In 1997, Louis Vuitton appointed Marc Jacobs as creative director. Jacobs brought a fresh perspective and experimented with new designs, collaborating with artists like Takashi Murakami and Stephen Sprouse to produce limited-edition collections that attracted younger consumers.

The brand's decision to collaborate with popular figures, such as Kanye West and Supreme, created buzz and rejuvenated the Louis Vuitton image. Louis Vuitton also took a bold step in expanding into digital marketing and e-commerce, modernizing its approach while maintaining its luxury status.

By repositioning itself as a brand that embraced modernity while maintaining its heritage, Louis Vuitton not only survived the counterfeit crisis but emerged even stronger, setting new standards for luxury fashion in the 21st century.

The Strategy:

1. Innovative Collaborations: Louis Vuitton partnered with contemporary artists and designers to create exclusive, limited-edition collections that appealed to younger generations while maintaining the brand's high-end status.
2. Embracing Digital Transformation: By incorporating e-commerce and digital marketing into its strategy, Louis Vuitton reached a broader audience and captured the attention of millennials and Gen Z customers.

3. Exclusivity and Limited Editions: The brand continued to leverage its heritage of craftsmanship while launching limited-edition products, making Louis Vuitton's products even more desirable and exclusive.
4. Revitalizing the Brand Image: Under Marc Jacobs, Louis Vuitton modernized its designs and marketing strategies, appealing to both traditional luxury consumers and a younger, trend-conscious audience.

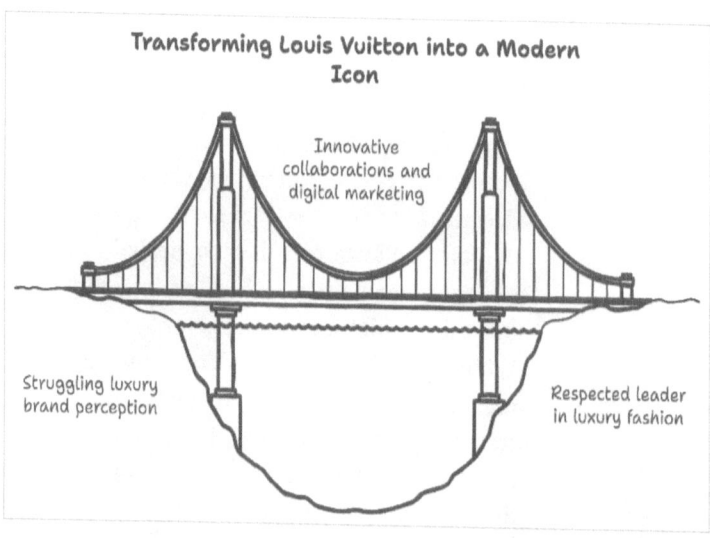

Key Takeaway:

"Louis Vuitton's success in overcoming the counterfeit crisis and reclaiming its position as an iconic luxury brand is a testament to the power of innovation, strategic collaborations, and an ability to adapt to changing consumer trends. By embracing modernity while staying true to its roots, Louis Vuitton turned adversity into an opportunity for reinvention."

Case 11: McDonald's Reinventing Fast Food

Introduction: McDonald's, founded in 1940 by Richard and Maurice McDonald, grew rapidly after Ray Kroc joined the company in 1954, transforming it into a global fast-food empire. By the 1990s, McDonald's had solidified its place as the largest and most recognizable fast-food chain in the world, with thousands of locations across the globe. Known for its burgers, fries, and soda, McDonald's became synonymous with fast, affordable, and satisfying meals.

The Problem: By the early 2000s, however, McDonald's faced significant challenges. The global rise in health consciousness, combined with rising concerns about obesity, led to growing criticism of McDonald's food offerings. The documentary Super-Size Me, released in 2004, showcased the dangers of consuming fast food regularly and became a cultural touchstone, amplifying negative perceptions about McDonald's food.

Sales began to drop as customers became more health-conscious, and the company's reputation for serving unhealthy, calorie-laden meals pushed it into a crisis. Furthermore, as fast-casual dining grew in popularity, McDonald's struggled to compete with brands offering fresher, healthier alternatives.

The Situation Becomes Worse: As McDonald's focused on its traditional menu, sales stagnated. Health-conscious consumers increasingly chose competitors like Subway, offering lower-calorie, "better-for-you" options. McDonald's also faced backlash over labor disputes, animal welfare, and environmental practices.

The brand's identity was under threat, struggling to align with changing preferences for healthier, sustainable food. McDonald's reliance on iconic items like the Big Mac and French fries felt outdated to a new generation demanding choice and transparency from supported brands.

The Breakthrough - Turning Adversity into Opportunity: McDonald's recognized the need for a radical shift in its offerings and image, innovating to embrace a healthier, sustainable future.

The company introduced healthier menu options like salads, fruit, and oatmeal, revamped cooking methods to include more grilled options, and launched the "lighter choices" menu, proving food could be tasty and healthy.

McDonald's also improved sustainability by sourcing sustainable ingredients, reducing its carbon footprint, and partnering with local farmers. Transparency became a focus, with nutritional information and ethical supply chain improvements addressing consumer demands for better food sourcing.

By 2015, the all-day breakfast menu became a customer favorite, demonstrating McDonald's ability to adapt to market demands. Expanding its digital presence with mobile ordering and delivery further emphasized convenience.

The brand repositioned itself as a leader in healthier living, sustainability, and innovation, catering to a diverse, health-conscious world.

The Strategy:

1. Healthier Menu Offerings: McDonald's incorporated healthier ingredients and options like salads, fruit, and grilled chicken to meet growing demand for nutritious food.
2. Sustainability Initiatives: The company improved its environmental practices, including sustainable sourcing, reducing food waste, and lowering its carbon footprint, addressing consumer concerns.
3. Brand Repositioning: McDonald's shifted its messaging to include healthier options and a focus on transparency, positioning itself as a forward-thinking brand.
4. Digital Transformation: The brand invested in mobile ordering and delivery, capitalizing on growing demand for convenience in the fast-food industry.

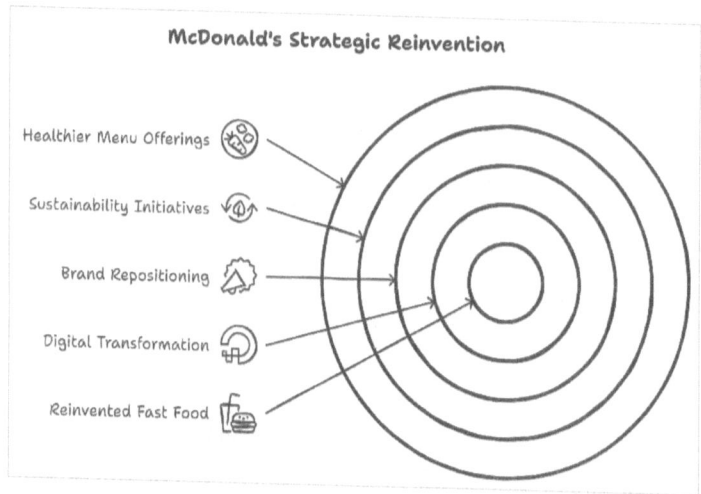

Key Takeaway

"McDonald's demonstrated that it is possible to turn around a crisis by embracing the changing market landscape. Through innovation, sustainability, and a commitment to healthier options, McDonald's reinvented itself and strengthened its brand identity, proving that adapting to adversity can lead to new growth opportunities."

Case 12:
Ford
Struggles to Success

Introduction: Ford Motor Company, founded by Henry Ford in 1903, revolutionized the automobile industry with the introduction of assembly-line manufacturing. By the mid-20th century, Ford was one of the "Big Three" automakers, producing millions of vehicles annually. However, by the early 2000s, the company faced significant financial challenges due to rising competition, shifting consumer preferences, and operational inefficiencies.

The Problem: In the early 2000s, Ford's market share was shrinking rapidly. The company was heavily reliant on gas-guzzling SUVs, which fell out of favor as fuel prices soared. Rising healthcare and pension costs for its employees further strained Ford's finances. By 2006, the company had posted a staggering $12.7 billion annual loss—the largest in its history. The global financial crisis loomed on the horizon, threatening to exacerbate the automaker's troubles.

The Situation Becomes Worse: The 2008 financial crisis hit the automotive industry hard. Ford's competitors, General Motors and Chrysler, sought government bailouts to stay afloat. Ford, too, faced the risk of bankruptcy. The company's reputation was in jeopardy, and consumer confidence in its ability to deliver quality products was waning. Compounding the crisis, Ford was burdened with outdated manufacturing processes and an unwieldy product lineup that failed to resonate with modern consumers. Analysts doubted the company's ability to survive without significant intervention.

The Breakthrough - Turning Adversity into Opportunity: Amidst the turmoil, Ford's newly appointed CEO, Alan Mulally, implemented a bold plan to save the company. Rejecting government bailout funds, Mulally focused on restructuring the company and reinvigorating its product lineup.

"One Ford" Vision: Mulally introduced the "One Ford" strategy, emphasizing a unified global product lineup. This approach eliminated redundancies and allowed the company to focus on producing fewer, higher-quality models that appealed to a global audience.

Securing Liquidity: Ford mortgaged nearly all of its assets, including the iconic blue oval logo, to secure $23.5 billion in loans. This bold move provided the liquidity needed to weather the financial crisis and invest in new technologies.

Product Innovation: Ford shifted its focus to fuel-efficient and eco-friendly vehicles, launching models like the Ford Fusion Hybrid and the Ford Fiesta. The company invested heavily in research and development to stay ahead of market trends.

Cost Efficiency: Ford streamlined its operations, closing underperforming plants and renegotiating labor agreements to reduce costs. The company also improved manufacturing efficiency, adopting lean production practices.

By 2009, Ford was the only U.S. automaker to avoid bankruptcy, emerging as a symbol of resilience in the industry. The company regained consumer trust and rebuilt its brand reputation, thanks to its focus on innovation, quality, and sustainability.

The Strategy:

1. Unified Vision: Implementing the "One Ford" strategy to streamline operations and create a cohesive global product lineup.
2. Bold Financial Moves: Mortgaging assets to secure funding and avoid reliance on government bailouts.
3. Consumer-Centric Products: Prioritizing fuel efficiency, sustainability, and modern designs to align with changing consumer preferences.
4. Operational Efficiency: Closing underperforming plants and renegotiating contracts to reduce costs and improve productivity.

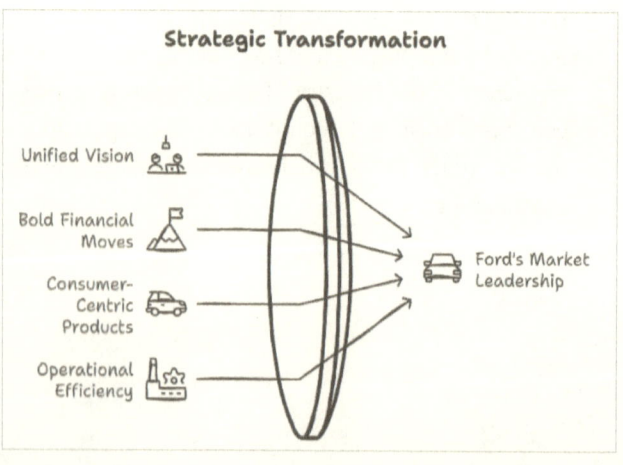

Key Takeaway

"Ford's story demonstrates the power of bold leadership and strategic focus. By turning financial and operational crises into opportunities for innovation and efficiency, Ford emerged stronger, proving that resilience and vision can transform adversity into long-term success."

Case 13:
Pfizer
Setbacks to Global Impact

Introduction: Pfizer, one of the world's leading pharmaceutical companies, has a long history of delivering life-saving medicines. Established in 1849, the company has pioneered numerous breakthroughs in medicine, including the development of antibiotics and vaccines. However, despite its successes, Pfizer faced significant challenges in the 2000s, including patent expirations, declining revenues, and intense competition in the pharmaceutical industry.

The Problem: By the mid-2010s, Pfizer's blockbuster drugs, including Lipitor (the best-selling cholesterol drug in history), faced patent expirations. Generic competitors quickly entered the market, leading to a steep decline in revenue. Simultaneously, the pharmaceutical industry faced growing regulatory scrutiny, rising R&D costs, and challenges in developing new, effective drugs. Pfizer needed to pivot quickly to ensure its future growth and relevance.

The Situation Becomes Worse: Pfizer's efforts to expand through acquisitions were met with resistance. The company's 2014 attempt to acquire AstraZeneca fell through, leaving Pfizer without a clear path to offset its declining revenues. Meanwhile, the R&D pipeline faced setbacks, with several high-profile drugs failing in late-stage clinical trials. The company's stock price stagnated, and investor confidence waned.

The Breakthrough - Turning Adversity into Opportunity: Amid challenges, Pfizer's leadership adopted a bold strategy emphasizing innovation, partnerships, and vaccines.

Strategic Partnerships: Pfizer's 2018 collaboration with BioNTech on mRNA technology became pivotal during the COVID-19 pandemic.

Diversification and Innovation: Investments in oncology, rare diseases, and vaccines led to breakthroughs like Ibrance (breast cancer) and the Prevnar vaccine.

Focus on Vaccines: During COVID-19, Pfizer and BioNTech developed the first mRNA-based vaccine, generating billions and addressing global health crises.

Operational Efficiency: Pfizer streamlined operations, divested its consumer health business, and refocused on biopharmaceuticals, improving margins and resource allocation.

Through agility and innovation, Pfizer turned challenges into success. Its COVID-19 vaccine saved millions and restored investor confidence.

The Strategy

1. Investing in Innovation: Leveraging emerging technologies like mRNA to address unmet medical needs.
2. Strategic Collaborations: Partnering with BioNTech to accelerate vaccine development.
3. Operational Streamlining: Divesting non-core businesses to focus on biopharmaceutical innovation.
4. Global Impact Focus: Addressing pressing global health challenges to build trust and relevance.

Key Takeaway

"Pfizer's journey highlights the value of adaptability and strategic foresight. By investing in innovation and partnerships, the company not only overcame its challenges but also made a lasting global impact, proving that adversity can catalyze extraordinary achievements."

Case 14: Google Search Engine Supremacy

Introduction: Google, now a household name, began its journey in 1998 as a small search engine startup co-founded by Larry Page and Sergey Brin. The company sought to organize the world's information and make it universally accessible. However, in its early days, Google faced skepticism, fierce competition, and financial challenges that threatened its very existence.

The Problem: In the late 1990s, search engines like Yahoo, AltaVista, and Lycos dominated the internet. Google was a newcomer in an already crowded space. Convincing investors and users to adopt their new algorithm-based search engine was an uphill battle. Additionally, Google struggled to generate revenue, leading to concerns about its sustainability.

The Situation Becomes Worse: Despite its superior search algorithm, Google lacked a viable monetization strategy. Early attempts, such as licensing its technology to other companies, failed to generate sufficient income. At the same time, competitors like Yahoo continued to dominate the market, making it difficult for Google to gain visibility. By 2001, the pressure to deliver profits intensified as the dot-com bubble burst, threatening the survival of internet-based companies.

The Breakthrough - Turning Adversity into Opportunity: Faced with challenges, Google's leadership made bold moves that changed its trajectory:

AdWords - Monetizing Search: In 2000, Google introduced AdWords, a revolutionary platform allowing businesses to place targeted ads based on search queries. Its pay-per-click model solved Google's revenue problem and set the foundation for financial success.

Focus on User Experience: Unlike competitors cluttered with ads, Google prioritized simplicity and speed, with its minimalist homepage attracting millions.

Technological Superiority: Google's refined PageRank algorithm delivered highly relevant results, cementing its reputation as a reliable search engine.

Global Expansion and Diversification: Google expanded beyond search into email (Gmail), video sharing (YouTube), and mobile platforms (Android), diversifying revenue streams and increasing dominance.

By the mid-2000s, Google had transformed into an internet powerhouse, its innovative model and user focus eclipsing competitors.

The Strategy:

1. Innovation in Monetization: Introducing AdWords to create a sustainable revenue model.
2. Customer-Centric Design: Prioritizing user experience with a clean and fast interface.
3. Relentless Innovation: Continuously improving its algorithm to maintain a competitive edge.
4. Strategic Diversification: Expanding into complementary tech services to ensure growth.

Key Takeaway

"Google's rise demonstrates the power of leveraging innovation to solve critical challenges. By aligning technology with user needs and monetization strategies, the company turned skepticism into dominance, setting a gold standard for businesses worldwide."

Case 15:
Patagonia
Conscious Business Icon

Introduction: Patagonia, the outdoor apparel company founded in 1973 by Yvon Chouinard, was built on a commitment to high-quality products and environmental stewardship. However, the company faced a significant crisis in the early 1990s when its rapid growth began to clash with its sustainability values.

The Problem: By the late 1980s, Patagonia's exponential growth brought unforeseen consequences. Manufacturing processes were linked to environmental degradation, and employee burnout was rampant due to the fast-paced work culture. Customers and stakeholders started questioning whether Patagonia could maintain its values while scaling its operations.

The Situation Becomes Worse: As scrutiny intensified, Patagonia discovered that the cotton used in its clothing was grown with harmful pesticides, contributing to environmental damage and violating its core values. Additionally, the stress from growth demands led to high turnover among employees, threatening the company's internal culture. Patagonia faced the harsh reality: continue growing unsustainably or take a bold stand to redefine its business model.

The Breakthrough - Turning Adversity into Opportunity: Instead of succumbing to pressure, Patagonia embraced its crisis as an opportunity to reinforce its mission:

Switch to Organic Cotton: In 1994, Patagonia committed to organic cotton despite higher costs and supplier resistance. This aligned its products with environmental values, setting a new industry standard.

Environmental Activism: Patagonia amplified advocacy through initiatives like "1% for the Planet," donating profits to environmental causes and educating customers about sustainability.

Employee-Centric Policies: To combat burnout, Patagonia introduced benefits like on-site childcare, flexible hours, and a four-day workweek. These measures fostered loyalty and workplace creativity.

Revolutionizing Consumer Behavior: Campaigns like "Don't Buy This Jacket" promoted conscious consumption, urging customers to repair rather than replace, resonating with environmentally conscious consumers and enhancing brand loyalty.

Patagonia thrived, becoming a leader in ethical business practices, proving profitability and purpose can coexist.

The Strategy

1. Commitment to Core Values: Prioritizing sustainability over short-term profits.
2. Proactive Advocacy: Using its platform to inspire environmental responsibility.
3. Employee Well-Being: Creating a supportive workplace to sustain long-term growth.
4. Transparency with Consumers: Educating and empowering customers to make sustainable choices.

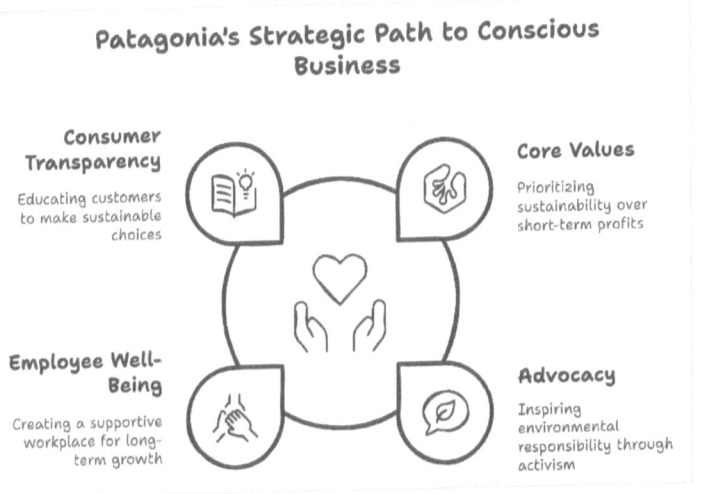

Key Takeaway

"Patagonia's journey shows how a company can turn adversity into an opportunity to lead by example. By aligning its operations with its core values, Patagonia redefined what it means to be a conscious business in the modern era."

Case 16:
Airbnb
Hospitality Disruption

Introduction: Airbnb started in 2008 when two roommates, Brian Chesky and Joe Gebbia, faced difficulty paying rent in San Francisco. They turned their living room into a makeshift bed-and-breakfast, offering air mattresses and breakfast to visitors. This humble idea laid the foundation for what would become a global hospitality giant.

The Problem: The early days of Airbnb were riddled with challenges. Skepticism surrounded the idea of strangers sharing their homes. Investors hesitated to back the concept, fearing a lack of trust and scalability. Moreover, traditional hospitality giants viewed Airbnb as a niche idea with no long-term viability.

The Situation Becomes Worse: In 2009, Airbnb nearly ran out of funds. Despite some users listing properties, the platform struggled to gain traction. Homeowners were wary of safety issues, while travelers doubted the reliability of such accommodations. With a limited budget and no significant user base, Airbnb was on the brink of collapse.

The Breakthrough - Turning Adversity into Opportunity: Rather than giving up, the founders implemented strategies to revitalize the business:

Perfecting the Platform: Chesky and Gebbia focused on user experience, improving listing quality by personally visiting hosts and ensuring professional property photographs attracted travellers.

Data-Driven Design: Analyzing user behavior, the team simplified booking, boosting conversions.

Crisis Marketing: During the 2008 recession, Airbnb positioned itself as a cost-effective travel alternative, appealing to both hosts and guests.

Creative Fundraising: Airbnb sold limited-edition cereal boxes during the 2008 U.S. presidential election, raising $30,000 and gaining media attention.

Building Trust: Introducing a robust review and verification system fostered trust between hosts and guests, pivotal for user adoption.

By 2011, Airbnb expanded to 89 countries, disrupting traditional hospitality and connecting millions of travelers with unique stays globally.

The Strategy

1. Understanding User Needs: Simplifying the platform and prioritizing trust-building features.
2. Creative Problem Solving: Using unconventional ideas (like the cereal campaign) to fund and promote the business.
3. Recession-Proof Model: Highlighting affordability during a global economic downturn.
4. Scalability: Streamlining operations to serve a global audience effectively.

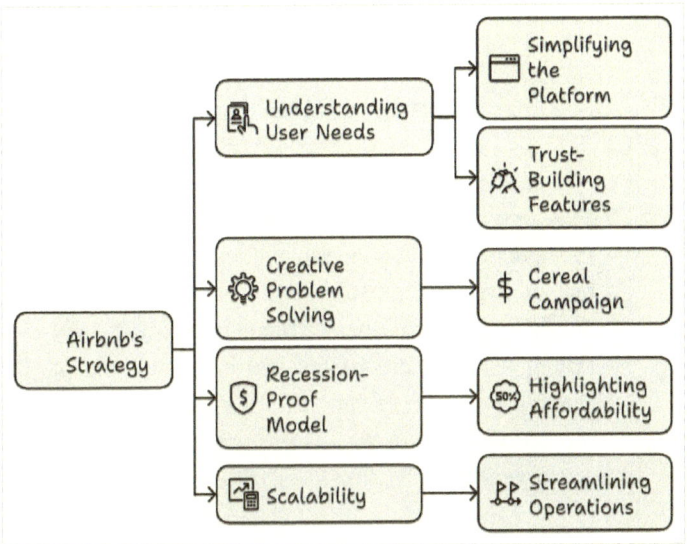

Key Takeaway

"Airbnb's rise shows that creative solutions, trust-building, and adaptability can transform even the simplest ideas into industry-disrupting giants."

Case 17:
Goldman Sachs
Scandal to Resilience

Introduction: Goldman Sachs, founded in 1869, is one of the most prestigious investment banks in the world, known for its financial prowess and influence. The firm has played a pivotal role in shaping global financial markets, but its reputation has been marred by scandal and controversy.

The Problem: The 2008 global financial crisis posed one of the biggest challenges to Goldman Sachs' legacy. The firm was accused of profiting from the housing market collapse by betting against mortgage-backed securities, while at the same time selling these risky investments to clients. This led to public outrage, with accusations that Goldman Sachs was contributing to the financial disaster, only to profit from the misfortune of others.

The Situation Becomes Worse: As the crisis deepened, Goldman Sachs found itself under intense scrutiny. Public trust in the firm evaporated, and its reputation took a severe hit. The U.S. government had to step in with a $10 billion bailout, which further tainted its image, leading to questions about the ethics of its business model.

The Breakthrough - Turning Adversity into Opportunity: Despite the scandal, Goldman Sachs navigated the crisis and restored its financial standing. Steps included:

Acknowledging the Crisis: Goldman Sachs admitted mistakes publicly, signaling a willingness to change and rebuilding stakeholder trust.

Reform and Regulation: The firm supported financial sector reforms, including the Dodd-Frank Act, promoting stability.

Adapting to a New Era: Post-crisis, Goldman Sachs shifted focus to sustainable, long-term investments, diversifying its portfolio with technology, data, and consumer banking.

Strong Leadership and Resilience: CEO Lloyd Blankfein restored company culture, emphasizing responsible practices, risk management, and transparency.

Corporate Social Responsibility: The firm rebuilt its image through philanthropy and responsible investing, supporting communities and sustainable projects.

Through these measures, Goldman Sachs regained confidence, emerging as a resilient player in global finance.

The Strategy

1. Accountability: Acknowledging mistakes and committing to transparency.
2. Diversification: Shifting focus from high-risk strategies to sustainable, long-term investments.
3. Leadership Resilience: Strong leadership and a commitment to reforming the company's culture and operations.
4. Adapting to Regulations: Embracing new financial regulations and supporting systemic reforms.

Key Takeaway

"Goldman Sachs' recovery from scandal teaches us that resilience, accountability, and a willingness to evolve can restore even the most tarnished brands to their former glory."

Case 18:
Gucci
Global Luxury Icon

Introduction: Gucci, founded in 1921 by Guccio Gucci in Florence, Italy, is one of the most iconic luxury brands in the world. Known for its high-end fashion, accessories, and leather goods, Gucci once faced severe financial turmoil and nearly went bankrupt in the 1990s. The brand, which had a rich legacy, was struggling to keep pace with changing market dynamics.

The Problem: In the early 1990s, Gucci was in disarray. The company was plagued by poor management, internal conflicts, and brand dilution. The lack of a cohesive vision, combined with financial mismanagement, led to a steep decline in brand value. Gucci's iconic products were becoming less relevant in the global market, and it lost touch with its core luxury audience.

The Situation Becomes Worse: In 1993, Gucci's financial crisis reached a boiling point, with the company teetering on the brink of bankruptcy. Its stock prices plunged, and internal power struggles led to the departure of key executives. The company had become a shadow of its former self, and even its once-celebrated products were no longer in demand. The brand was struggling to maintain its status as a luxury powerhouse.

The Breakthrough - Turning Adversity into Opportunity: Gucci's revival is a remarkable example of brand reinvention. In 1994, bringing Tom Ford as creative director marked a dramatic transformation:

Tom Ford's Vision: Ford introduced bold, provocative designs that restored Gucci's exclusivity and desirability. His glamorous, edgy collections attracted younger, affluent customers craving modern luxury.

Brand Reinvention: Under Ford, Gucci redefined its image, moving away from outdated 1980s designs to a contemporary, edgy aesthetic. High-quality craftsmanship reinvigorated Gucci's legendary leather goods.

Global Expansion: Expanding into Asia and the Middle East and opening flagship stores globally solidified Gucci's status as a global luxury leader.

Celebrity Endorsement: Celebrity endorsements by icons like Jennifer Lopez, Gwyneth Paltrow, and Madonna elevated Gucci's visibility and reinforced its luxury status.

Sustainability and Innovation: Gucci embraced sustainability, sourcing eco-friendly materials and reducing its carbon footprint, appealing to conscious luxury consumers.

By the late 1990s, Gucci had regained its position as a leading luxury brand, continuing its resurgence with innovation and quality.

The Strategy

1. Bold Creative Vision: Tom Ford's fresh approach to fashion and design helped Gucci regain its luxury status.
2. Brand Reinvention: Reconnecting with high-end consumers through contemporary, edgy aesthetics.
3. Strategic Expansion: Expanding into new global markets and opening flagship stores in key cities.

4. Celebrity Endorsement: Utilizing celebrity power to reinforce brand image.
5. Sustainability: Committing to sustainable practices, appealing to modern, eco-conscious luxury consumers.

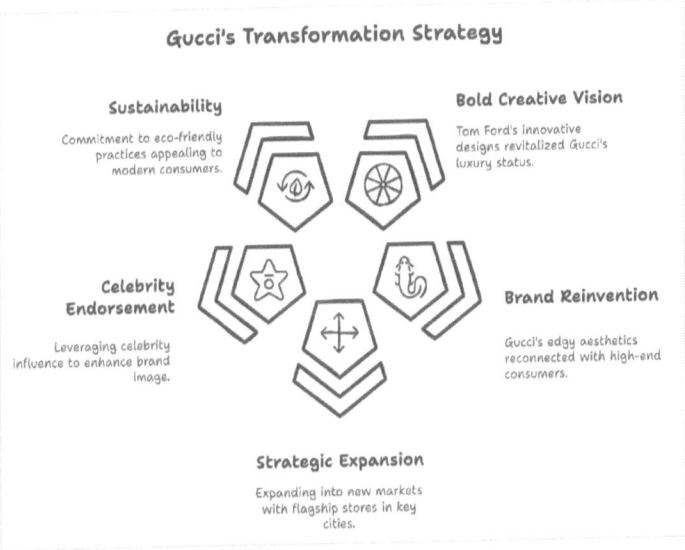

Key Takeaway

"Gucci's remarkable turnaround highlights the importance of innovation, brand reinvention, and aligning with shifting consumer values to revive a once-diluted brand."

Case 19:
Spotify
Music Streaming Empire

Introduction: Spotify, launched in 2008 by Daniel Ek and Martin Lorentzon in Sweden, started as a music streaming service in a market dominated by piracy and illegal downloads. The music industry was grappling with plummeting sales due to rampant piracy, and Spotify aimed to provide a legal alternative by offering access to millions of songs through a subscription-based model.

The Problem: Spotify's biggest challenge was the music industry's reluctance to embrace streaming. Record labels were initially skeptical, worried that streaming services would cannibalize their existing revenue models. At the same time, Spotify faced stiff competition from other music platforms, and many users still preferred illegal downloads, which seemed easier and free. Additionally, Spotify was burning through cash, and the model of offering free and premium subscriptions was not generating enough revenue to cover licensing costs and operational expenses.

The Situation Becomes Worse: By 2010, Spotify was struggling to maintain its business model. The company faced challenges in securing long-term licensing agreements with major record labels. Despite having a growing user base, it was not making any profit and was heavily reliant on venture capital funding to stay afloat. To make matters worse, piracy was still rampant, and Spotify's success depended heavily on convincing users to pay for subscriptions instead of relying on free or illegal alternatives.

The Breakthrough - Turning Adversity into Opportunity: Spotify's breakthrough came through a series of strategic decisions that focused on creating a unique user experience, expanding globally, and adapting to market changes:

Licensing Deals with Major Labels: Spotify was able to negotiate favorable licensing deals with major record labels by offering them a revenue-sharing model. These deals ensured that Spotify could provide a vast music catalog while also compensating artists and labels fairly. These strategic partnerships allowed Spotify to legally stream music, giving it credibility and building trust with users.

Freemium Model: Spotify's innovative "freemium" business model – offering a free, ad-supported version of its service alongside a premium, subscription-based service – helped grow its user base. Users who enjoyed the free version could then be converted into paying customers, thereby boosting Spotify's revenue stream.

Personalized Recommendations and Playlists: One of Spotify's key differentiators became its ability to personalize music for users. By using algorithms and user data, Spotify provided personalized playlists like Discover Weekly, which helped users discover new music based on their preferences. This increased user engagement and retention.

Expansion into Global Markets: Spotify aggressively expanded into international markets, particularly in Europe, the U.S., and later, emerging markets like India. This global expansion gave Spotify access to a vast audience and helped it capture a significant share of the global streaming market.

Strategic Acquisitions and Partnerships: Spotify continued to innovate through strategic acquisitions, including buying podcast platforms like Anchor and Gimlet Media. This expanded Spotify's content offering, attracting new users and enhancing its position in the growing podcast market.

By 2018, Spotify achieved a milestone of 200 million active users, and it continued to grow, offering new features like podcasts and social integration, securing its place as the world's leading music streaming service.

The Strategy

1. Securing Licensing Deals: Negotiated with major record labels to create a vast music catalog.
2. Freemium Model: Introduced a free version with ads and a premium subscription model.
3. Personalization: Developed algorithms to create customized playlists for users.
4. Global Expansion: Entered multiple international markets to increase its global footprint.
5. Content Diversification: Acquired podcast platforms to offer new forms of content.

Key Takeaway

"Spotify's success lies in its ability to adapt to market changes, innovate continuously, and offer value through personalized, accessible, and diversified content."

Case 20: Coca-Cola Reigniting Growth

Introduction: Coca-Cola, founded in 1886, is one of the world's most iconic brands, recognized for its flagship soft drink. For decades, Coca-Cola enjoyed unparalleled success, dominating the global beverage market. However, in the 2000s, the company faced serious challenges in a rapidly evolving market with changing consumer preferences, increased health consciousness, and declining soda sales in key markets like the U.S.

The Problem: By the early 2010s, Coca-Cola's growth had stalled. Its core product – Coca-Cola Classic – was facing reduced demand as consumers began shifting towards healthier alternatives like bottled water, juices, and sports drinks. Additionally, the rise of local competitors offering cheaper options, combined with health warnings about sugary drinks, led to a perception crisis for Coca-Cola. The company was also grappling with market saturation in developed countries, where almost every household already had access to the product.

The Situation Becomes Worse: Despite aggressive marketing campaigns, Coca-Cola struggled to maintain its market share. Its flagship soda was facing significant sales decline, and attempts to diversify into health-conscious drinks (like diet sodas) failed to resonate with a new generation of consumers. Furthermore, its dependence on carbonated drinks, a shrinking market segment, left the company vulnerable to shifting tastes and growing competition from brands like PepsiCo and new-age beverage companies.

The Breakthrough - Turning Adversity into Opportunity: Coca-Cola's revival stemmed from rethinking its strategy, diversifying its portfolio, and adapting to changing consumer demands:

Diversification of Product Portfolio: Coca-Cola expanded beyond sodas, acquiring brands like Minute Maid, Honest Tea, and Costa Coffee. This diversification catered to health-conscious consumers seeking non-carbonated alternatives.

Health-Conscious Focus: The company reduced sugar content, launched smaller portions, and introduced Coca-Cola Zero Sugar to appeal to calorie-conscious groups, broadening its consumer base.

Innovative Marketing Campaigns: Campaigns like "Share a Coke" personalized experiences, driving emotional engagement and boosting sales, especially among younger consumers.

Global Expansion: Coca-Cola focused on emerging markets like Africa and Asia, leveraging growing beverage demand and its strong brand presence for revenue growth.

Sustainability: Coca-Cola emphasized eco-friendly initiatives like water stewardship and sustainable packaging, improving public perception and resonating with environmentally-conscious consumers.

By the mid-2010s, Coca-Cola had transformed into a diversified global beverage powerhouse, driven by innovation, health-consciousness, and sustainability.

The Strategy

1. Product Diversification: Acquired brands in non-carbonated and healthy beverage categories.
2. Health-Conscious Innovation: Reduced sugar content and introduced healthier alternatives.

3. **Effective Marketing Campaigns:** Personalized and emotionally engaging campaigns like "Share a Coke."
4. **Expansion into Emerging Markets:** Focused on fast-growing regions like Africa and Asia.
5. **Sustainability Focus:** Invested in environmental initiatives and corporate social responsibility.

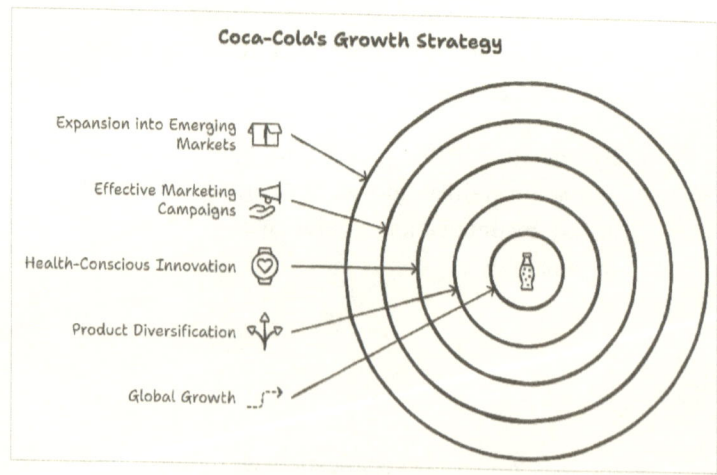

Key Takeaway

"Coca-Cola's ability to reinvent itself by embracing new consumer preferences, diversifying its offerings, and staying committed to sustainability helped it rise from a market saturation crisis to global dominance."

Case 21: Costco Thriving with Uniqueness

Introduction: Costco, a membership-based warehouse retailer, was founded in 1983 in the United States. It quickly became one of the largest retailers globally, known for its unique business model that combines low prices with limited selection. Costco's strategy centers around providing bulk products at discounted prices, often in a no-frills, warehouse-style shopping experience. Despite being in an intensely competitive retail environment dominated by giants like Walmart and Amazon, Costco has carved out a successful niche and sustained impressive growth.

The Problem: In the 1990s and early 2000s, as the retail industry became more competitive and the shift towards e-commerce began, Costco's business model was under pressure. The low-margin, bulk-selling approach was challenging to sustain in a market increasingly driven by convenience, branding, and the rise of online shopping. On top of this, Costco's business relied heavily on its membership model, which meant it needed to ensure a continuous stream of customers who would pay an annual fee for the privilege of shopping at its warehouses.

The Situation Becomes Worse: While Costco's physical stores flourished, its e-commerce presence was relatively underdeveloped, and the company was losing out to competitors like Amazon, which offered convenience, home delivery, and a vast product selection. The members-only model, while offering exclusive pricing, was also a limiting factor, especially in a world that increasingly valued convenience over cost savings. This led to concerns over how Costco would compete with a rising tide of online retailers and changing consumer expectations.

The Breakthrough - Turning Adversity into Opportunity: Costco leaned into its strengths, focusing on value and evolving to thrive in retail:

Refining the Membership Model: Costco enhanced its membership benefits, offering discounts, exclusive products, and excellent service, creating a "club with perks" experience.

Focus on Bulk and Value: By negotiating lower supplier prices and curating a smaller selection, Costco provided unmatched bulk-buying value, appealing to cost-conscious customers, especially during downturns.

Strategic Expansion into E-Commerce: Costco developed an online shopping option while maintaining a strong in-store focus, differentiating itself from Amazon's wide selection.

Global Expansion and Localization: Entering markets in Asia, Europe, and Latin America, Costco localized product offerings and store layouts to suit regional preferences.

Supply Chain Efficiency: Tight supply chain control and long-term supplier relationships ensured low costs and exclusive member deals. By doubling down on bulk value and adapting strategically, Costco thrived amid retail challenges.

The Strategy

1. Leveraging the Membership Model: Continued to emphasize membership value, making it feel like an exclusive club.
2. Focus on Bulk and Savings: Positioned as the go-to retailer for bulk products at discounted prices.
3. E-commerce Adaptation: Gradually built an online presence, complementing the in-store experience.

4. **International Expansion with Local Adaptation:** Expanded globally with market-specific strategies.
5. **Operational Efficiency and Vendor Relationships:** Focused on maintaining low costs and securing favorable vendor deals.

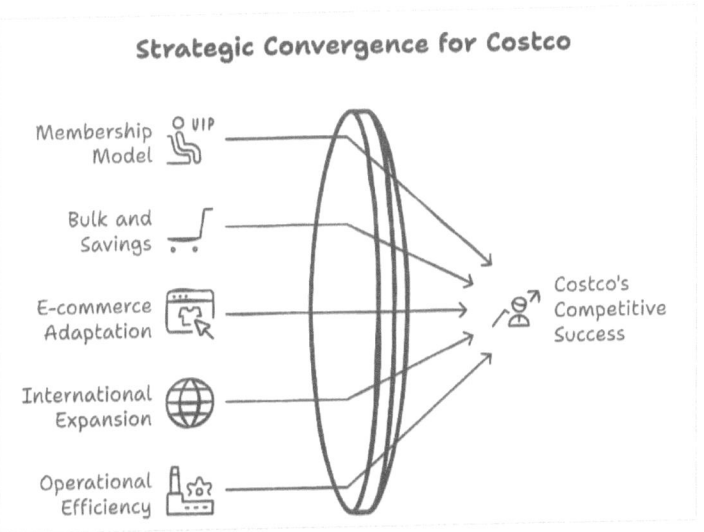

Key Takeaway

"Costco's strategy of focusing on value, operational efficiency, and selective global expansion allowed it to stand firm against competition, even in the face of changing consumer preferences and the rise of online retail."

Case 22:
JPMorgan
Financial Crisis to Strength

Introduction: JPMorgan Chase, one of the largest and most prestigious financial institutions globally, has long been a symbol of financial strength and stability. With a history dating back over 200 years, the bank has weathered numerous financial storms, including the 2008 global financial crisis. Known for its investment banking, asset management, and consumer banking services, JPMorgan Chase has positioned itself as a leader in the financial sector.

The Problem: The 2008 global financial crisis marked a turning point for JPMorgan Chase. As the subprime mortgage market collapsed, financial institutions worldwide faced severe losses. Banks, including JPMorgan, were heavily exposed to risky mortgage-backed securities and credit default swaps. The crisis caused a widespread liquidity freeze, pushing the global economy to the brink of collapse. JPMorgan faced exposure to troubled assets, a declining stock price, and a trust crisis in the financial industry.

The Situation Becomes Worse: As the financial crisis deepened, JPMorgan's stock price plummeted, and the bank was forced to write off billions of dollars in bad loans. The entire banking industry was in turmoil, and JPMorgan was not immune. In an effort to stabilize the economy, the U.S. government intervened, providing financial assistance to banks, including JPMorgan. However, despite the government bailout, the bank's reputation was severely tarnished, and it faced a crisis of confidence from investors and customers. The situation grew worse as the full scale of the global recession became evident, and financial markets continued to be volatile.

The Breakthrough - Turning Adversity into Opportunity: While the financial crisis initially pushed JPMorgan Chase to the brink, the leadership under CEO Jamie Dimon took decisive actions that helped the bank not only survive but thrive in the years that followed:

Strategic Acquisitions: One of JPMorgan's key strategies during the crisis was to take advantage of the opportunities presented by the financial turmoil. The bank acquired Bear Stearns and Washington Mutual, two failing financial institutions. These acquisitions were risky, but they provided JPMorgan with valuable assets, including a significant increase in market share and the ability to absorb troubled companies at a relatively low cost. These moves were critical to JPMorgan's recovery.

Strengthening Risk Management: In response to the crisis, JPMorgan Chase made significant improvements in its risk management strategies. The bank revamped its approach to evaluating risk, focusing on minimizing exposure to high-risk assets. By introducing more robust risk controls and ensuring a more diversified portfolio, JPMorgan was able to weather future financial storms more effectively. This restructuring helped restore confidence in the bank and positioned it to manage future challenges more effectively.

Doubling Down on Core Business: While other banks were focused on high-risk investments, JPMorgan refocused its attention on its core business—consumer banking, investment banking, and asset management. By narrowing its focus and concentrating on what it did best, JPMorgan Chase regained stability and profitability. This strategy not only helped the bank recover from the crisis but also allowed it to strengthen its position in the global banking industry.

Focusing on Innovation: Another key factor in JPMorgan's recovery was its commitment to innovation. The bank invested heavily in technology and digital banking solutions, positioning itself as a leader in the fintech space. JPMorgan became one of the first banks to develop advanced online and mobile banking services, making banking more convenient for customers and attracting a new generation of tech-savvy consumers.

Building Trust with Customers: JPMorgan understood that rebuilding trust after the crisis would be essential to its recovery. The bank worked hard to improve customer relations, focusing on transparency, accountability, and integrity. By rebuilding trust with customers and investors, JPMorgan was able to regain its position as one of the most respected financial institutions in the world.

By focusing on strategic acquisitions, strengthening its risk management, doubling down on its core businesses, and embracing innovation, JPMorgan Chase was able to emerge from the 2008 financial crisis stronger than ever. The company's ability to adapt to the changing financial landscape and focus on long-term growth set it apart from many of its competitors.

The Strategy

1. Strategic Acquisitions: Acquired Bear Stearns and Washington Mutual, increasing market share and assets.
2. Strengthening Risk Management: Improved risk assessment protocols and diversified its portfolio.
3. Doubling Down on Core Business: Focused on consumer banking, investment banking, and asset management.
4. Innovation in Technology: Invested in digital banking and fintech to lead in the innovation space.
5. Building Customer Trust: Worked on rebuilding trust through transparency and better customer relations.

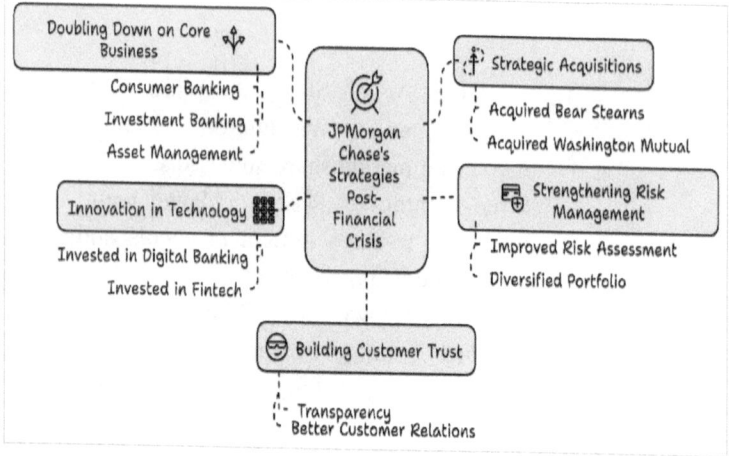

Key Takeaway

"JPMorgan Chase turned the 2008 financial crisis into an opportunity for growth by making bold acquisitions, strengthening its core business, embracing innovation, and rebuilding trust with customers."

Case 23:
Samsung
Hardship to Leadership

Introduction: Samsung, a global leader in electronics and technology, has built an empire spanning smartphones, televisions, semiconductors, and consumer appliances. Founded in 1938 in South Korea, the company quickly grew into a major player in various industries. However, it wasn't always smooth sailing for Samsung. The company faced a major crisis in the early 2010s that could have derailed its growth and market dominance.

The Problem: In 2010, Samsung faced intense competition from Apple in the smartphone market. Apple revolutionized the industry with the iPhone, becoming synonymous with innovation and high-quality design. Samsung, despite its technological expertise, struggled with product aesthetics and consumer loyalty. Its mobile division suffered from sluggish sales, limited differentiation, and a tarnished image, with market share eroding and its reputation at stake.

The Situation Becomes Worse: In 2011, Samsung faced another blow when it was sued by Apple for patent infringement, specifically accusing the company of copying its design and features. This legal battle dragged on for years, negatively impacting Samsung's brand image. As the lawsuit gained media attention, Samsung's smartphone business saw a decline in sales, and there were concerns within the company about whether it could ever regain its position in the market. With Apple continuing to dominate and the ongoing legal battles, Samsung's future appeared uncertain.

The Breakthrough - Turning Adversity into Opportunity: Despite mounting challenges, Samsung's leadership under Chairman Lee Kun-hee viewed the crisis as an opportunity to reinvent the company. Rather than succumbing to setbacks, Samsung made strategic moves to solidify its position as a global tech leader.

Innovation and Design Focus: Samsung focused on innovation and design, launching the Galaxy series with advanced hardware, larger screens, and enhanced features, helping it compete with Apple and capture market attention.

Aggressive Marketing and Branding: Samsung positioned itself as Apple's challenger, highlighting its devices' larger screens, customization options, and multitasking capabilities through high-profile campaigns, winning over younger consumers.

Expanding Product Ecosystem: By integrating products like TVs, tablets, and wearables, Samsung created a seamless ecosystem, reinforcing its brand's appeal and innovation.

Investing in R&D: Samsung prioritized cutting-edge technology like 5G, AI, and foldable smartphones, pushing industry boundaries and introducing game-changing products.

Strong Leadership and Long-Term Vision: Chairman Lee's focus on quality, innovation, and global expansion guided Samsung's turnaround, prioritizing long-term growth over short-term gains.

Through innovation, marketing, ecosystem diversification, and R&D, Samsung overcame its crisis and reemerged as a global tech leader.

The Strategy

1. Product Innovation and Design: Launched the Galaxy series with cutting-edge technology and improved aesthetics.
2. Aggressive Marketing: Focused on differentiating its smartphones from Apple's and promoting its unique features.
3. Expanding Product Ecosystem: Developed a seamless ecosystem across smartphones, TVs, home appliances, and wearables.
4. R&D Investment: Prioritized technological advancements in 5G, AI, and foldable smartphones.
5. Strong Leadership: Visionary leadership focused on long-term goals and resilience.

Key Takeaway

"Samsung turned adversity into opportunity by reinventing its brand with innovation, expanding its product ecosystem, and staying committed to long-term growth."

Case 24:
Intel
Disruption to Dominance

Introduction: Intel, founded in 1968, has long been a global leader in semiconductor manufacturing. The company revolutionized the personal computing industry with its microprocessors and quickly became the standard in computing hardware. For decades, Intel's dominance in the microprocessor market was unrivalled, powering personal computers, laptops, and servers around the world. However, in the mid-2010s, Intel faced significant challenges that threatened to erode its market leadership.

The Problem: Intel's strength was in microprocessor technology, but the rise of mobile computing, particularly smartphones and tablets, shifted the landscape. Intel was slow to adapt, focusing on PCs and data centers. Meanwhile, ARM Holdings gained market share, and competitors like AMD caught up with powerful processors.

Intel's manufacturing processes, once an advantage, fell behind due to delays in production technology. In 2020, AMD surpassed Intel in performance per watt efficiency in the consumer PC market, signaling the end of Intel's dominance.

The Situation Becomes Worse: As Intel struggled to deliver its next-generation chips, it started facing a severe credibility crisis. Competitors like AMD and ARM-based processors gained significant traction in mobile devices, while Intel's offerings in mobile chips were practically nonexistent. The company's market share began to slip, and its once dominant position in the CPU market was under threat. Moreover, delays in Intel's chip production process meant that it could not meet customer demand for the latest technology, damaging its relationship with key clients like Apple, who began seeking alternatives. Intel's market value dropped, and many questioned whether it could return to its former glory.

The Breakthrough - Turning Adversity into Opportunity: Despite challenges, Intel's leadership under CEO Pat Gelsinger (who returned in 2021) made decisions that helped the company regain its competitive edge. Intel's strategy shifted dramatically to adapt to new market realities.

Revamping Manufacturing Processes: Intel focused on its core strength—semiconductor manufacturing—investing billions to improve chip-making facilities and align with industry leaders like TSMC. The company committed to 7nm and 5nm processes to stay competitive, maintaining control over production for high-performance chips.

Investing in New Markets: Intel expanded into AI, automotive, and cloud computing, focusing on chips for AI workloads, autonomous vehicles, and IoT devices. Acquisitions like Mobileye positioned Intel as a key player in future technological ecosystems.

Partnerships with Competitors: In a shift from its traditional strategy, Intel began partnering with competitors, offering manufacturing services to rivals like AMD and Apple. This move positioned Intel as a leading chip-making provider globally.

Leadership and Vision: Pat Gelsinger reinvigorated Intel's commitment to innovation and long-term growth, focusing on cloud computing, AI, and autonomous vehicles. Intel's shift to innovation allowed it to regain market confidence.

Through cutting-edge manufacturing, strategic diversification, and partnerships, Intel turned its crisis into opportunity, regaining its position as a key semiconductor industry player.

The Strategy

1. Revamping Manufacturing: Reinvested in semiconductor fabrication to catch up with the industry's leading chip makers.
2. Diversification into New Markets: Expanded into AI, autonomous driving, and IoT by acquiring key companies like Mobileye.
3. Strategic Partnerships: Opened up Intel's foundries to external clients, offering chip manufacturing services to competitors.
4. Strong Leadership: Leadership under Pat Gelsinger focused on long-term growth, innovation, and diversification.

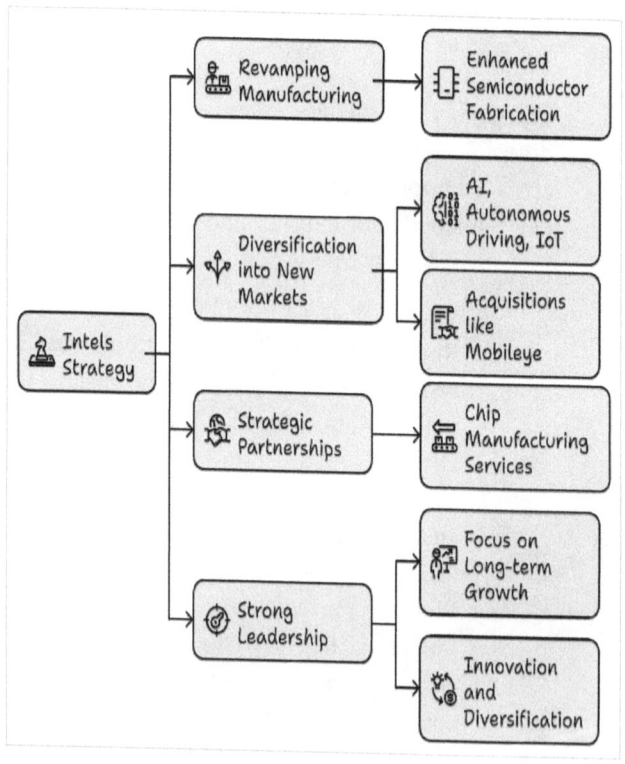

Key Takeaway:

Intel reinvented itself by focusing on technological innovation, strategic diversification, and partnerships, ensuring its relevance in the fast-evolving semiconductor industry.

Case 25:
LEGO
Building Blocks of Success

Introduction: LEGO, the world-renowned Danish toy manufacturer, has been delighting children and adults alike for decades with its iconic interlocking plastic bricks. Founded in 1932, LEGO built a strong legacy as the creative building block that encouraged imagination and problem-solving. But despite its enduring popularity, the company faced one of its greatest crises in the early 2000s.

The Problem: By the early 2000s, LEGO's leadership began facing the harsh reality that the toy industry was changing. Kids were spending more time on video games and other digital entertainment, leaving traditional toys like LEGO sets less appealing. The company's reliance on its classic sets became a liability as it failed to adapt quickly to new trends. LEGO also expanded into areas like clothing, theme parks, and video games, but this diversification created operational inefficiencies and failed to capture new customers. LEGO's sales began to fall, and the company's brand started to lose its cultural relevance.

The Situation Becomes Worse: In 2003, LEGO faced a near-catastrophic crisis. The company reported significant losses, and its once-proud position in the global toy market was in jeopardy. A focus on non-core products like video games and clothing distracted LEGO from its roots—building blocks. Meanwhile, competitors started creating their own versions of building toys, with cheaper, more accessible alternatives to LEGO. Internal problems—such as mismanagement, supply chain inefficiencies, and poor product development—only compounded the issue. The company's future was uncertain, and many wondered if LEGO could recover.

The Breakthrough - Turning Adversity into Opportunity: In the face of this adversity, LEGO turned to its core strength: creativity. A leadership change in 2004 brought Jørgen Vig Knudstorp into the CEO role. Knudstorp, who had deep insights into LEGO's culture and operations, recognized that the company needed to return to its roots creating a brand that fostered imagination, creativity, and play.

Refocusing on Core Products: Knudstorp made the bold decision to cut down on non-core products and refocus on the iconic LEGO brick. This meant discontinuing certain product lines that were not aligned with the company's values, including clothes, video games, and other licensed products. By simplifying its offerings, LEGO could focus on improving the quality and innovation of its beloved building sets.

Innovation through Licensing: One of the most successful strategies that LEGO implemented was collaborating with popular franchises. LEGO partnered with well-established brands like Star Wars, Harry Potter, and Marvel, creating themed building sets that combined the creativity of LEGO with the global appeal of these franchises. These sets attracted older audiences who grew up with LEGO but had drifted away as they entered adulthood. This partnership allowed LEGO to re-establish its relevance in a rapidly changing market, as kids were drawn to both the LEGO brand and their favorite movie or TV franchises.

Engaging with the Fan Community: LEGO also began to engage directly with its passionate fanbase. The company created LEGO Ideas, a platform that allowed fans to submit their own designs for sets, with the potential for these ideas to become official products. This gave LEGO enthusiasts a voice in product development and ensured the brand stayed in touch with its core customer base. The company also created LEGO Masters, a TV show that brought the fun and creativity of LEGO building to a global audience, further increasing its popularity.

Embracing Digital Trends: LEGO embraced digital trends, too, by launching digital play experiences, including mobile apps, video games, and augmented reality experiences. This integration of physical and digital play appealed to the younger generation who were more tech-savvy, and the company started to bridge the gap between traditional toys and modern entertainment.

Through these strategic decisions, LEGO not only stabilized but also grew, and it transformed from a company on the brink of collapse to one of the most influential toy brands in the world. LEGO had proven that by staying true to its core values while adapting to the times, a company could survive and thrive even in the face of adversity.

The Strategy

1. Refocused on Core Strengths: Shifted focus back to LEGO bricks and streamlined product offerings to reduce operational inefficiencies.
2. Innovative Licensing Partnerships: Collaborated with major brands like Star Wars, Harry Potter, and Marvel to create popular themed sets.
3. Engagement with Fans: Launched LEGO Ideas to allow fans to submit their own designs for new sets, creating a sense of community.
4. Embraced Digital Play: Integrated digital experiences such as mobile apps, video games, and augmented reality with the physical LEGO sets to appeal to a new generation.

Key Takeaway

"LEGO's resurgence demonstrates that staying true to your core while embracing new opportunities for innovation and engagement can lead to unprecedented success, even after facing near collapse."

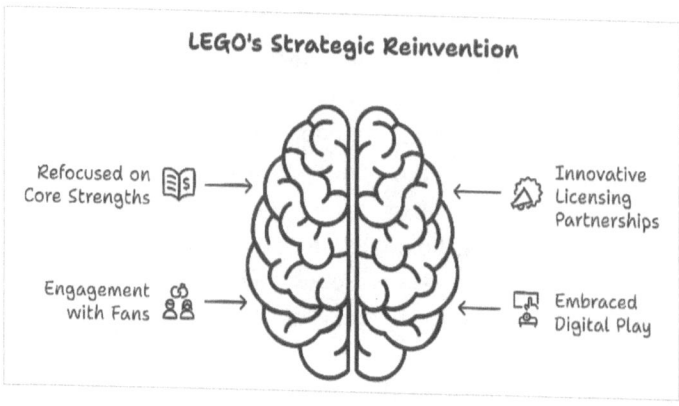

Case 26:
eBay
Obsolescence to Leader

Introduction: eBay, founded in 1995 by Pierre Omidyar, was originally conceived as an online auction platform where individuals could buy and sell products. eBay rapidly gained popularity, becoming a pioneer in e-commerce. By the early 2000s, it was seen as the go-to online marketplace, connecting millions of buyers and sellers around the world. However, despite its early success, eBay faced a major crisis in the following decade, threatening its position as a market leader.

The Problem: By the mid-2000s, eBay's dominance in the e-commerce space was beginning to erode. Online shopping habits were changing, and new competitors, such as Amazon, were making rapid advances. While eBay had once been a marketplace where individuals could auction off items, it was struggling to adapt to the shift towards fixed-price, instant purchases. Additionally, the platform became flooded with counterfeit and low-quality goods, leading to a deterioration in customer trust and satisfaction.

eBay's focus on auctions limited its ability to compete against Amazon's fast-growing and user-friendly online store.

The Situation Becomes Worse: As the years went by, eBay's growth stagnated. Competitors like Amazon had mastered the art of offering a wide range of products at fixed prices with reliable shipping and customer service. Meanwhile, eBay's auction model, which had been central to its success, seemed outdated. The influx of subpar sellers and products only exacerbated The Problem. eBay's user base, once loyal, started to dwindle, and the company's market share in e-commerce fell.

The company's stock price plummeted, and many analysts predicted eBay's eventual decline. The leadership at eBay realized they needed to rethink their strategy or face extinction.

The Breakthrough - Turning Adversity into Opportunity: In 2008, eBay underwent a major leadership change with John Donahoe taking over as CEO. He realized that eBay's future didn't lie in competing with Amazon head-on in the retail space but in reinventing itself as a marketplace for consumer-to-consumer transactions. He spearheaded a major overhaul to revitalize eBay's platform, addressing its weaknesses head-on.

Transition to Fixed-Price Listings: Instead of relying solely on auctions, eBay introduced more fixed-price listings, allowing sellers to offer products at a set price. This move helped eBay better compete with Amazon and other retail giants that provided a more convenient shopping experience.

Improved Seller and Buyer Trust: eBay invested heavily in improving its buyer and seller protections, focusing on creating a safer and more reliable marketplace. With the introduction of eBay Buyer Protection and the implementation of better feedback systems, the company restored trust among customers and helped encourage repeat business.

Mobile Commerce and Global Expansion: eBay also embraced the rise of mobile commerce. With the launch of its mobile app and better integration of mobile shopping features, eBay capitalized on the increasing use of smartphones for shopping. The company expanded its global presence, reaching customers and sellers in international markets, further solidifying its position as a major player in the e-commerce industry.

Acquisitions to Boost Capabilities: To support its transformation, eBay made strategic acquisitions, including the purchase of PayPal in 2002, which became a crucial part of its ecosystem, offering secure payment solutions. eBay also acquired other e-commerce and marketplace platforms like StubHub and a significant share of the online classified ads market, diversifying its portfolio.

Through these changes, eBay was able to reinvent itself and reclaim its leadership position. While Amazon continued to dominate in the retail space, eBay managed to carve out its niche as a global marketplace for secondhand goods, collectibles, and unique items.

The Strategy

1. Shift to Fixed-Price Listings: Introduced fixed-price sales alongside auctions to appeal to modern shopping preferences.
2. Enhanced Buyer and Seller Trust: Focused on buyer protection policies and seller ratings to ensure a reliable marketplace.
3. Embraced Mobile Commerce: Launched a mobile app and optimized the platform

for mobile devices to capture the growing mobile shopping trend.
4. Global Expansion: Expanded internationally and optimized its platform to serve customers in diverse markets around the world.
5. Strategic Acquisitions: Acquired companies like PayPal and StubHub to strengthen its marketplace ecosystem and payment capabilities.

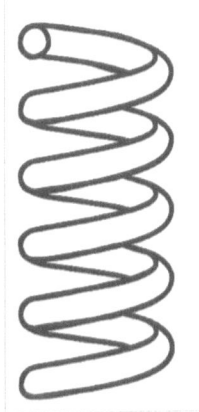

eBay's Transformation Strategy

 Shift to Fixed-Price Listings

 Enhanced Buyer and Seller Trust

 Embraced Mobile Commerce

 Global Expansion

 Strategic Acquisitions

Key Takeaway

"eBay's journey highlights the importance of adapting to changing market trends, rebuilding trust, and leveraging technology to remain relevant. By focusing on what made it unique and evolving its offerings, eBay turned its adversity into opportunity, ensuring its place in the global e-commerce landscape."

Case 27:
Delta
Leading the Skies

Introduction: Delta Airlines, founded in 1924, is one of the major airlines in the United States, with a reputation for offering extensive domestic and international flights. For decades, it was one of the leaders in the airline industry. However, by the early 2000s, Delta faced a significant crisis that threatened its survival in an increasingly competitive and volatile market.

The Problem: Delta's troubles began with the global airline industry crisis post-9/11, which severely impacted travel demand. At the same time, rising fuel prices and intense competition from low-cost carriers like Southwest and Spirit Airlines put tremendous pressure on Delta's financial health. Despite being a large, established company, Delta was burdened with high operating costs, outdated technology, and an inefficient fleet. In 2005, Delta filed for bankruptcy, marking a crucial low point in its history.

The Situation Becomes Worse: While filing for bankruptcy offered Delta a chance to restructure, the company struggled with an image crisis. Passengers were increasingly choosing low-cost carriers for short-haul flights, and Delta's high prices and outdated services were losing customers. Even worse, Delta's leadership faced criticism for not moving quickly enough to modernize the airline and address the mounting operational inefficiencies.

By 2007, Delta was still in a precarious financial position. With competition ramping up and customer expectations rising, the airline was at risk of losing its position as a leader in the industry. The once-glorious brand was facing an existential crisis.

The Breakthrough - Turning Adversity into Opportunity: In 2008, Delta Airlines made a bold move by merging with Northwest Airlines, creating the world's largest airline. This merger provided Delta with an opportunity to cut costs, expand its network, and streamline operations. But there was still a long road ahead.

Rebuilding Trust with Customers: Delta took immediate steps to improve its customer service.

From investing in a more modern fleet to revamping its frequent flyer program, Delta began to rebuild its reputation with travellers. It also worked to enhance its in-flight services, focusing on improving comfort, connectivity, and convenience for passengers. The airline's "Customer First" initiative aimed to create a personalized experience for travellers, ensuring they felt valued at every touchpoint.

Embracing Technology: Delta recognized the importance of technology in modernizing the airline experience. The company invested heavily in tech innovations, including a state-of-the-art booking system, advanced mobile applications, and improved baggage tracking. Delta's use of technology streamlined operations, enhanced customer experience, and optimized its entire flight network.

Focus on Operational Efficiency: Delta implemented a series of cost-cutting measures and operational changes to improve efficiency. The airline streamlined its fleet by retiring older planes and replacing them with more fuel-efficient models. It also focused on reducing delays, increasing on-time arrivals, and improving overall operational performance.

Sustainability and Corporate Responsibility: Delta Airlines committed to sustainability, setting ambitious goals for reducing its carbon footprint. This not only enhanced its reputation as a responsible corporation but also aligned with a growing consumer preference for environmentally conscious brands. Delta's focus on sustainability helped the company appeal to the new wave of eco-aware travelers.

By the mid-2010s, Delta had fully recovered from its bankruptcy days and became one of the most profitable and admired airlines in the industry. Its revenue increased, its customer loyalty grew, and it expanded its global reach, becoming a dominant player in the international airline market.

The Strategy

1. Merger for Growth: Delta's strategic merger with Northwest Airlines expanded its network and allowed it to consolidate resources.
2. Customer-Centric Approach: Revitalized its customer service programs to focus on enhancing the passenger experience and fostering loyalty.

3. Embracing Technology: Invested in technology for booking systems, mobile apps, and baggage handling to improve both operations and customer satisfaction.
4. Cost-Efficiency and Fleet Modernization: Streamlined its fleet, improved fuel efficiency, and implemented cost-cutting measures to increase profitability.
5. Commitment to Sustainability: Adopted sustainability practices to reduce its environmental impact and appeal to a more eco-conscious customer base.

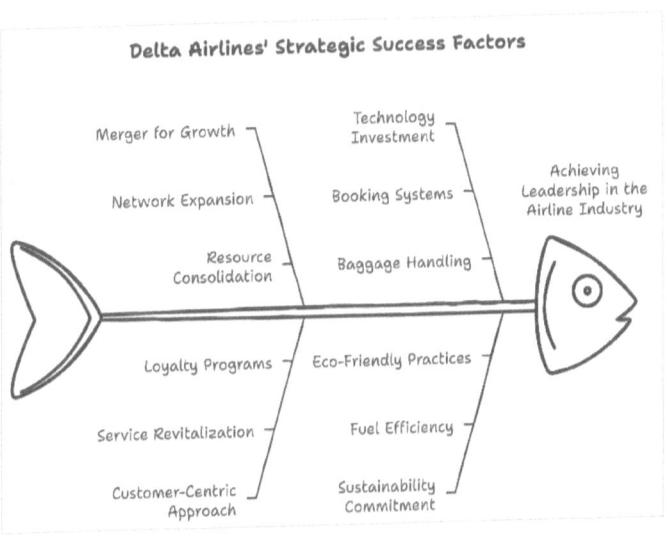

Key Takeaway

"Delta Airlines' story is a powerful reminder that even in times of crisis, companies that focus on innovation, customer satisfaction, and operational efficiency can emerge stronger. By embracing change and learning from adversity, Delta not only survived but thrived, redefining itself as a leader in the competitive airline industry."

Case 28:
IBM
Adversity to Tech Powerhouse

Introduction: IBM, originally known as International Business Machines, was once a giant in the computing industry. Founded in 1911, it dominated the world of mainframes and personal computers, playing a key role in the development of computing hardware and software. However, by the late 1990s, IBM faced a crisis of relevance as the market shifted toward personal computers and software solutions.

The Problem: In the 1990s, IBM's core business model was increasingly outdated. The company had become too reliant on its hardware business, especially mainframe computers, which were no longer in high demand. As personal computers began to take over, and software companies like Microsoft and Intel emerged as market leaders, IBM found itself struggling to adapt. Despite having a strong legacy, it faced shrinking profits, a saturated market, and increasing competition from other tech companies.

The Turning Point came when IBM's stock price began to drop, and it became clear that the company's traditional business approach was no longer viable. Investors and analysts started questioning whether IBM could remain a leader in the industry or if it would become obsolete.

The Situation Becomes Worse: By 1993, IBM was at a crossroads. The company had already seen its market share slip, and its traditional business units were no longer driving growth. In an effort to combat its financial troubles, IBM laid off tens of thousands of employees and tried restructuring its operations. However, the company continued to face a series of challenges, including slow sales, massive internal inefficiencies, and a lack of direction in the rapidly changing tech landscape.

The Breakthrough - Rebuilding from Scratch: Rather than continuing to fight a losing battle, IBM decided to reinvent itself. Under CEO Lou Gerstner, who took over in 1993, IBM embarked on a journey of transformation that would position it for success.

Shifting Focus from Hardware to Services and Software: Gerstner's key strategy was shifting IBM's focus from hardware to services and software. This departure from the traditional business model allowed IBM to tap into the growing IT services market. IBM invested heavily in consulting, enterprise software, cloud computing, and business analytics.

Acquiring Key Technologies: To strengthen its new focus, IBM made strategic acquisitions, including PwC Consulting in 2002 and Red Hat in 2019. These moves helped IBM expand its footprint in cloud computing and AI, allowing it to compete with tech giants like Google, Amazon, and Microsoft.

Embracing Cloud Computing and AI: IBM's focus on artificial intelligence (AI) and cloud computing was key to its revival. By investing in Watson AI and hybrid cloud solutions, IBM positioned itself at the forefront of technological advancement. Watson became known for its success in natural language processing and data analytics, making IBM a trusted partner for organizations seeking AI solutions.

Rebranding and Reshaping the Company's Image: As part of its reinvention, IBM rebranded as a technology-driven solutions provider, focusing on innovation, R&D, and thought leadership. IBM became recognized for its leadership in AI, quantum computing, and cybersecurity, while maintaining its position as a tech giant.

By the 2010s, IBM successfully transitioned from hardware to a more profitable business model centered on services, software, and cutting-edge technologies.

The Strategy

1. Shift to Services and Software: Focused on transforming IBM into a services and software company by de-emphasizing hardware.
2. Strategic Acquisitions: Acquired key companies such as PwC Consulting and Red Hat to strengthen its software and cloud computing divisions.
3. Embrace of Emerging Technologies: Invested in artificial intelligence (AI), cloud computing, and quantum computing to stay ahead of industry trends.
4. Rebranding Efforts: Focused on reshaping its image and positioning itself

as a technology solutions provider, especially in AI and cloud computing.

Key Takeaway:

"IBM's story is a prime example of how even the most established companies can rise from the ashes of adversity by embracing change, investing in future technologies, and reinventing themselves. By shifting its focus from hardware to services, software, and cutting-edge technologies, IBM became a leader in the digital transformation era."

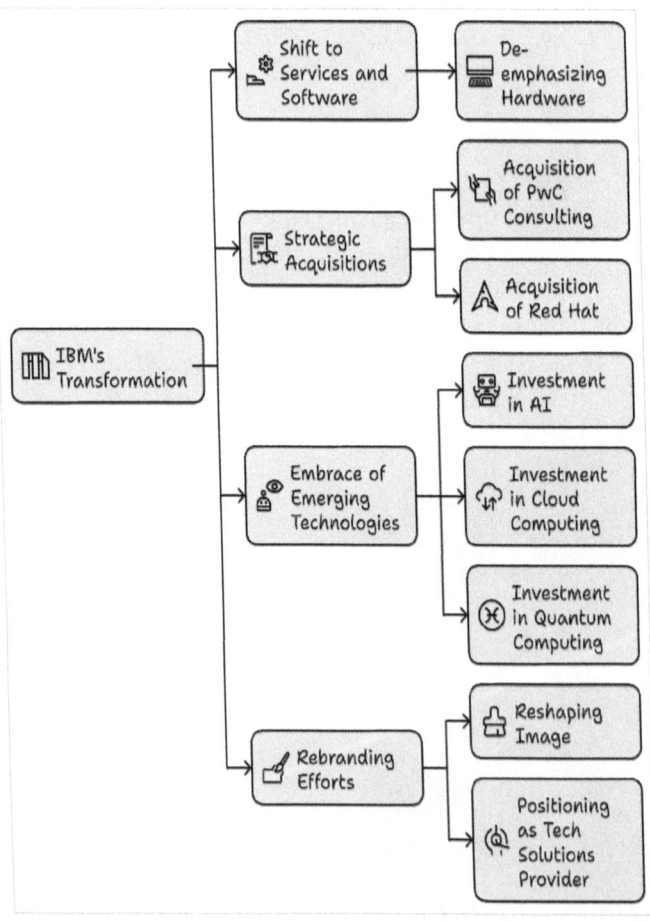

Case 29: Alibaba Global E-Commerce Empire

Introduction: Alibaba, founded by Jack Ma in 1999, started as a small e-commerce platform connecting Chinese manufacturers with overseas buyers. Born in the city of Hangzhou, Alibaba's story was not one of instant success. Jack Ma, who had no background in technology or business, struggled to get investors on board, and many people doubted his ability to turn his idea into a global giant. However, Ma's persistence and belief in the power of the internet and e-commerce ultimately revolutionized global trade.

The Problem: In the early days, Alibaba faced enormous challenges. The concept of online commerce was relatively new in China, and the internet infrastructure was not as developed as it is today. Even more challenging was the fact that Jack Ma had to compete with established international players like eBay, Amazon, and other Western e-commerce giants.

The biggest problem Alibaba faced was credibility. In a country like China, where trust was a major issue in online transactions, Ma had to convince buyers and sellers to use his platform. The risk of fraud was a significant concern, and many believed that e-commerce would never work in China due to the cultural and logistical barriers.

The Situation Becomes Worse: The challenges compounded when Alibaba's early years were marked by financial struggles. Ma faced resistance from investors, and the company struggled to generate profits. Critics argued that Alibaba's business model wouldn't work, especially with high competition from global players like eBay. Internet penetration in China was low, and many consumers were skeptical of buying products online due to lack of robust payment systems and logistical infrastructure.

In 2003, things worsened when eBay, already dominant, entered China with eBay China, aiming to take over the local e-commerce market. However, Jack Ma decided to double down on his belief that Alibaba could beat eBay.

The Breakthrough - Innovating to Win: Instead of directly competing with eBay, Alibaba created a unique value proposition tailored to the local market. Here are key strategies Jack Ma used to turn Alibaba into an e-commerce powerhouse:

Alipay – Building Trust in Online Transactions: In 2004, Alibaba launched Alipay, a third-party payment system acting as an escrow service, holding the buyer's money until the goods were received and inspected. This reduced fraud risk and built trust.

Focus on the B2B Market: Alibaba initially focused on B2B rather than eBay's C2C model, connecting small businesses in China with international buyers, helping Alibaba become the go-to platform for global sourcing.

Expanding into E-Commerce Platforms: In 2003, Alibaba launched Taobao, a C2C platform to compete with eBay China. Unlike eBay, Taobao didn't charge listing fees, making it more accessible. This led to eBay pulling out of China in 2006.

Technological Innovations and Global Expansion: Alibaba expanded into cloud computing (Alibaba Cloud), digital entertainment, and logistics, becoming the world's largest e-commerce platform by GMV. Strategic investments and the rise of the Chinese middle class helped maintain dominance.

By 2014, Alibaba became one of the largest companies in the world, setting a record for the largest IPO at the time. Jack Ma's bold vision had come to fruition.

The Strategy:

1. Trust and Payment Solutions – Alipay: Built trust by offering a payment system that protected both buyers and sellers.
2. B2B Focus Before B2C – Targeting Businesses: Started with B2B to build a strong foundation before moving to B2C.
3. No Listing Fees – Taobao's Advantage: Allowed free listings for individual sellers, attracting millions of small businesses.
4. Diversification – Beyond E-Commerce: Expanded into cloud computing, digital entertainment, and logistics to capture a larger global market share.
5. Global Expansion – Growth Beyond China: Initially focused on China, later expanding internationally to lead the global e-commerce market.

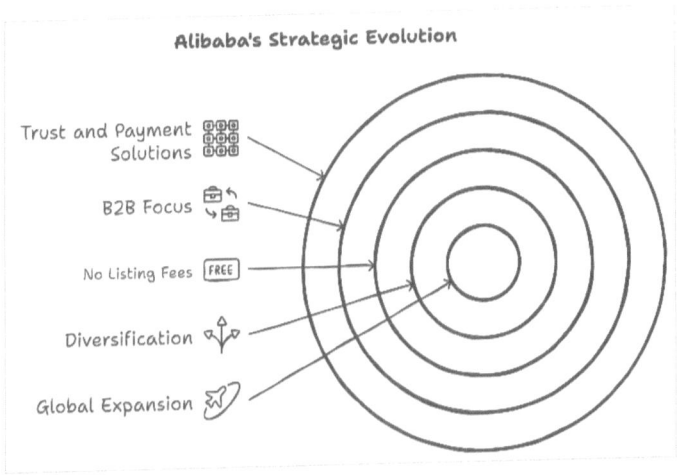

Key Takeaway

"Alibaba's story highlights the importance of innovation, adaptability, and a customer-first mindset in overcoming adversity. By creating a unique value proposition and adapting its model to the local market, Alibaba not only survived but thrived, becoming a dominant force in global e-commerce."

www.ingramcontent.com/pod-product-compliance
Lightning Source LLC
Chambersburg PA
CBHW031417210526
45464CB00005B/1931